50 Thailand Cake Recipes for Home

By: Kelly Johnson

Table of Contents

- Pad Thai
- Green Curry
- Tom Yum Goong (Spicy Thai Soup with Shrimp)
- Massaman Curry
- Som Tum (Green Papaya Salad)
- Pad Krapow Moo (Thai Basil Pork)
- Pad See Ew (Stir-Fried Noodles)
- Tom Kha Gai (Chicken Coconut Soup)
- Panang Curry
- Khao Pad (Thai Fried Rice)
- Larb (Spicy Thai Salad)
- Gaeng Keow Wan Gai (Thai Green Chicken Curry)
- Pad Pak Bung Fai Daeng (Stir-Fried Morning Glory)
- Pad Prik Khing (Stir-Fried Green Beans with Red Curry Paste)
- Pad Grapow Gai (Stir-Fried Chicken with Holy Basil)
- Moo Ping (Thai Grilled Pork Skewers)
- Gai Pad Med Mamuang (Stir-Fried Chicken with Cashew Nuts)
- Pla Rad Prik (Fried Fish with Chili Sauce)
- Thai Crab Fried Rice
- Khao Soi (Northern Thai Curry Noodles)
- Yum Woon Sen (Thai Glass Noodle Salad)
- Pad Ped Moo Pa (Spicy Jungle Curry with Pork)
- Pad Thai Jay (Vegetarian Pad Thai)
- Khao Niew Mamuang (Thai Mango Sticky Rice)
- Khao Soi Gai (Northern Thai Coconut Curry Noodle Soup with Chicken)
- Kai Med Ma Muang (Chicken with Cashew Nuts)
- Pad Preaw Wan Gai (Sweet and Sour Chicken)
- Gaeng Panang Neua (Panang Beef Curry)
- Pla Kapong Neung Manao (Steamed Fish with Lime)
- Pla Tod Rad Prik (Fried Fish with Chili Sauce)
- Gai Yang (Thai Grilled Chicken)
- Kao Pad Tom Yum Goong (Tom Yum Fried Rice with Shrimp)
- Pad Khing Sod Gai (Stir-Fried Chicken with Ginger)
- Tom Klong Pla Kra Phong (Thai Spicy Sour Sea Bass Soup)
- Pad Ped Pla Dook (Spicy Catfish Stir-Fry)

- Gaeng Som (Thai Sour Curry)
- Kaeng Khiao Wan Kai (Thai Green Chicken Curry)
- Yum Talay (Spicy Thai Seafood Salad)
- Pla Nueng Manao (Steamed Fish with Lime and Chili)
- Pad Phak Boong Fai Daeng (Stir-Fried Morning Glory with Chili and Soy Bean Sauce)
- Pad Mee Korat (Spicy Stir-Fried Noodles from Korat)
- Khao Pad Sapparod (Pineapple Fried Rice)
- Khao Pad Gai (Thai Chicken Fried Rice)
- Pad Thai Thale (Seafood Pad Thai)
- Kao Pad Goong (Shrimp Fried Rice)
- Gaeng Som Pla (Thai Spicy and Sour Fish Curry)
- Pad Pak Ruam (Stir-Fried Mixed Vegetables)
- Kai Jeow (Thai Omelette)
- Pad Cha (Spicy Stir-Fry with Thai Herbs)
- Khao Mun Gai (Thai Chicken Rice)

Pad Thai

Ingredients:

For the Pad Thai:

- 8 oz (225g) rice noodles (preferably flat noodles)
- 8-10 large shrimp, peeled and deveined (or substitute with chicken, tofu, or more vegetables)
- 2 eggs
- 1 cup firm tofu, cut into small cubes
- 2 cloves garlic, minced
- 1 shallot, finely chopped
- 1 cup bean sprouts
- 4 green onions, sliced into 1-inch pieces
- 1/4 cup roasted peanuts, finely chopped
- 2 tablespoons vegetable oil
- Lime wedges, for serving
- Fresh cilantro, chopped, for garnish

For the Pad Thai Sauce:

- 3 tablespoons tamarind paste
- 3 tablespoons fish sauce
- 2 tablespoons soy sauce
- 1 tablespoon rice vinegar
- 3 tablespoons brown sugar
- 1/2 teaspoon chili flakes (adjust to taste)

Instructions:

1. **Prepare the rice noodles:**
   - Soak the rice noodles in warm water for about 30 minutes, or until they are pliable but still firm. Drain well and set aside.
2. **Make the Pad Thai sauce:**
   - In a small bowl, whisk together the tamarind paste, fish sauce, soy sauce, rice vinegar, brown sugar, and chili flakes until the sugar is dissolved. Adjust sweetness or saltiness to taste.
3. **Cook the protein and tofu:**
   - Heat 1 tablespoon of vegetable oil in a large wok or skillet over medium-high heat. Add the shrimp (or chicken/tofu) and cook until pink and cooked through, about 2-3 minutes per side. Remove from the pan and set aside.
4. **Stir-fry the aromatics:**
   - In the same wok or skillet, add another tablespoon of oil. Add minced garlic and chopped shallot, and stir-fry for about 1 minute until fragrant.

5. **Add eggs and scramble:**
    - Push the aromatics to one side of the pan. Crack the eggs into the empty space and scramble them until they are cooked through.
6. **Combine noodles and sauce:**
    - Add the soaked and drained rice noodles to the wok or skillet. Pour the prepared Pad Thai sauce over the noodles and gently toss everything together until well combined and heated through.
7. **Add vegetables and protein:**
    - Add the cooked shrimp (or chicken/tofu) back into the pan, along with bean sprouts and sliced green onions. Stir-fry for another 1-2 minutes until everything is heated through.
8. **Serve:**
    - Transfer the Pad Thai to serving plates. Sprinkle with chopped roasted peanuts and garnish with fresh cilantro.
9. **Garnish and serve:**
    - Serve Pad Thai hot, garnished with lime wedges on the side. Enjoy your homemade Pad Thai!

Tips:

- Adjust the level of spiciness by adding more or less chili flakes or serving with additional chili sauce.
- For a vegetarian version, omit the shrimp and use tofu or simply add more vegetables.
- Customize Pad Thai with your favorite toppings such as extra lime wedges, cilantro, or crushed peanuts.

This recipe captures the authentic flavors of Pad Thai, making it a delicious and satisfying dish to enjoy with family and friends.

Green Curry

Ingredients:

For the Green Curry Paste:

- 4-6 green Thai chilies, deseeded for milder heat (adjust to taste)
- 2 shallots, chopped
- 4 cloves garlic, minced
- 1 stalk lemongrass, thinly sliced (white part only)
- 1 thumb-sized piece of galangal, sliced (or substitute with ginger)
- 1 teaspoon ground coriander
- 1/2 teaspoon ground cumin
- 1/2 teaspoon shrimp paste (optional, omit for vegetarian)
- 1 tablespoon fresh cilantro roots or stems, chopped
- Zest of 1 lime
- 1 tablespoon fish sauce (or soy sauce for vegetarian)
- 1 teaspoon brown sugar
- 1/2 cup fresh Thai basil leaves (or regular basil leaves)
- 2-3 tablespoons vegetable oil

For the Curry:

- 1 lb (450g) chicken breast or thighs, thinly sliced (or substitute with tofu, shrimp, or vegetables)
- 1 can (14 oz) coconut milk
- 1 cup chicken broth (or vegetable broth)
- 1 red bell pepper, sliced
- 1 cup Thai eggplant, halved (or substitute with regular eggplant)
- 1 cup bamboo shoots, sliced (canned, drained)
- 2 kaffir lime leaves, torn (optional, for authentic flavor)
- 1 tablespoon fish sauce (or soy sauce for vegetarian)
- 1 tablespoon palm sugar (or brown sugar)
- Fresh Thai basil leaves, for garnish

Instructions:

1. **Prepare the Green Curry Paste:**
   - In a food processor or blender, combine green Thai chilies, shallots, garlic, lemongrass, galangal (or ginger), ground coriander, ground cumin, shrimp paste (if using), cilantro roots or stems, lime zest, fish sauce, and brown sugar.
   - Process until a smooth paste forms, adding vegetable oil gradually to help blend the ingredients smoothly.
2. **Cook the Curry:**

- In a large skillet or wok, heat 2 tablespoons of vegetable oil over medium-high heat. Add 2-3 tablespoons of the green curry paste (store any remaining paste in an airtight container in the refrigerator for up to 1 week).

3. **Sauté the Curry Paste:**
   - Stir-fry the curry paste for 1-2 minutes until fragrant.
4. **Add Coconut Milk and Chicken:**
   - Pour in the coconut milk and chicken broth. Stir to combine and bring to a gentle simmer.
5. **Simmer the Curry:**
   - Add the sliced chicken (or protein of choice) to the simmering curry. Cook for 5-7 minutes, stirring occasionally, until the chicken is cooked through.
6. **Add Vegetables:**
   - Add the sliced red bell pepper, Thai eggplant, bamboo shoots, and torn kaffir lime leaves (if using).
7. **Season the Curry:**
   - Stir in fish sauce (or soy sauce) and palm sugar (or brown sugar). Adjust seasoning to taste.
8. **Simmer Further:**
   - Continue to simmer the curry for another 5-10 minutes, or until the vegetables are tender and flavors are well combined.
9. **Garnish and Serve:**
   - Remove from heat and stir in fresh Thai basil leaves. Garnish with additional basil leaves.
10. **Serve:**
    - Serve hot with steamed jasmine rice or rice noodles. Enjoy the aromatic and flavorful Green Curry!

Tips:

- Adjust the spiciness of the curry by adding more or fewer green Thai chilies.
- For a vegetarian or vegan option, use tofu or substitute with mixed vegetables like bell peppers, eggplant, and bamboo shoots.
- Kaffir lime leaves and Thai basil contribute to the authentic flavor of Green Curry but can be omitted or substituted with lime zest and regular basil if unavailable.

This homemade Green Curry recipe allows you to enjoy the bold flavors of Thai cuisine in the comfort of your home. It's perfect for a flavorful dinner with friends and family!

Tom Yum Goong (Spicy Thai Soup with Shrimp)

Ingredients:

For the Soup Base:

- 4 cups chicken or vegetable broth
- 2 cups water
- 2 stalks lemongrass, smashed and cut into 2-inch pieces
- 4-5 kaffir lime leaves, torn into pieces
- 3-4 slices galangal (or ginger, thinly sliced)
- 3-4 Thai bird's eye chilies, smashed (adjust to taste)
- 2 cloves garlic, smashed
- 1 medium-sized tomato, quartered
- 1 small onion, quartered
- 1 tablespoon fish sauce
- 1 tablespoon tamarind paste (or lime juice)
- 1 teaspoon sugar
- Salt, to taste

For the Tom Yum Goong:

- 10-12 large shrimp (prawns), peeled and deveined
- 1 cup button mushrooms, sliced
- 1/2 cup cherry tomatoes, halved
- 2-3 tablespoons lime juice (adjust to taste)
- Fresh cilantro leaves, chopped, for garnish
- Thai bird's eye chilies, sliced (optional, for extra heat)
- Fresh Thai basil leaves, for garnish (optional)

Instructions:

1. **Prepare the Soup Base:**
   - In a large pot, combine chicken or vegetable broth and water. Add lemongrass, kaffir lime leaves, galangal (or ginger), smashed Thai bird's eye chilies, and smashed garlic. Bring to a boil over medium-high heat.
2. **Simmer the Soup Base:**
   - Once boiling, reduce heat to medium-low and let it simmer for about 10-15 minutes to allow the flavors to infuse into the broth.
3. **Add Aromatics and Vegetables:**
   - Add quartered tomato, quartered onion, fish sauce, tamarind paste (or lime juice), and sugar to the pot. Stir well and continue to simmer for another 5 minutes.
4. **Cook the Shrimp:**
   - Add peeled and deveined shrimp (prawns) to the simmering broth. Cook for 2-3 minutes until the shrimp turn pink and are cooked through.

5. **Add Mushrooms and Tomatoes:**
    - Stir in sliced mushrooms and halved cherry tomatoes. Cook for another 2-3 minutes until mushrooms are tender.
6. **Adjust Seasoning:**
    - Taste the soup and adjust seasoning with fish sauce, lime juice, and salt as needed. Adjust the spiciness by adding more smashed Thai bird's eye chilies if desired.
7. **Serve:**
    - Remove the soup from heat. Discard lemongrass, galangal slices, smashed garlic, and any remaining kaffir lime leaves (if preferred).
8. **Garnish and Serve:**
    - Ladle the hot Tom Yum Goong into serving bowls. Garnish with fresh cilantro leaves, sliced Thai bird's eye chilies (if desired), and Thai basil leaves.
9. **Enjoy:**
    - Serve immediately as a flavorful and aromatic soup. Enjoy Tom Yum Goong with steamed jasmine rice or as a standalone dish.

Tips:

- For a vegetarian version (Tom Yum Hed), substitute shrimp with tofu or mixed vegetables like mushrooms, carrots, and bell peppers.
- Adjust the level of spiciness by adding more or fewer Thai bird's eye chilies.
- Fresh ingredients like lemongrass, kaffir lime leaves, and galangal are key to the authentic flavors of Tom Yum Goong. If unavailable, you can substitute with dried versions, but adjust quantities accordingly.

This homemade Tom Yum Goong recipe captures the essence of Thai cuisine with its spicy, sour, and fragrant flavors. It's perfect for warming up on a chilly day or as a refreshing soup any time of year.

Massaman Curry

Ingredients:

For the Massaman Curry Paste:

- 5-6 dried red chilies, soaked in warm water to soften
- 1 tablespoon coriander seeds
- 1 teaspoon cumin seeds
- 1/2 teaspoon whole cloves
- 1/2 teaspoon ground nutmeg
- 1/2 teaspoon ground cinnamon
- 1 teaspoon shrimp paste (optional, omit for vegetarian)
- 1/2 teaspoon ground white pepper
- 1 teaspoon ground cardamom
- 1 teaspoon ground turmeric
- 4-5 shallots, peeled and chopped
- 4 cloves garlic, peeled
- 1 thumb-sized piece of galangal, peeled and chopped (or substitute with ginger)
- 1 stalk lemongrass, thinly sliced (white part only)
- Zest of 1 lime
- 1 tablespoon vegetable oil
- 1 tablespoon tamarind paste (or substitute with lime juice)
- 1 tablespoon palm sugar (or brown sugar)
- 1 tablespoon fish sauce (or soy sauce for vegetarian)

For the Massaman Curry:

- 1 lb (450g) beef (such as stewing beef), cut into bite-sized cubes (can also use chicken or tofu)
- 1 can (14 oz) coconut milk
- 1 cup chicken broth (or vegetable broth)
- 2-3 medium potatoes, peeled and cut into chunks
- 1 onion, sliced
- 1/2 cup roasted peanuts
- 2-3 kaffir lime leaves, torn into pieces (optional, for authentic flavor)
- 1 cinnamon stick
- 2 tablespoons vegetable oil
- 1 tablespoon massaman curry paste (from above, adjust to taste)
- 1 tablespoon tamarind paste (or substitute with lime juice)
- 1 tablespoon fish sauce (or soy sauce for vegetarian)
- 1 tablespoon palm sugar (or brown sugar)
- Fresh cilantro leaves, chopped, for garnish
- Cooked jasmine rice, for serving

Instructions:

1. **Prepare the Massaman Curry Paste:**
   - In a dry skillet, toast coriander seeds, cumin seeds, and whole cloves over medium heat until fragrant, about 1-2 minutes. Remove from heat and let cool.
   - In a food processor or mortar and pestle, grind the toasted spices together with ground nutmeg, ground cinnamon, ground white pepper, ground cardamom, and ground turmeric until fine.
   - Add softened dried red chilies (remove seeds for less heat), shrimp paste (if using), chopped shallots, peeled garlic cloves, chopped galangal (or ginger), thinly sliced lemongrass (white part only), and lime zest. Process or grind until a smooth paste forms, adding vegetable oil gradually to help blend.
   - Stir in tamarind paste (or lime juice), palm sugar (or brown sugar), and fish sauce (or soy sauce). Adjust seasoning to taste.
2. **Cook the Massaman Curry:**
   - In a large pot or Dutch oven, heat 2 tablespoons of vegetable oil over medium-high heat. Add 1 tablespoon of Massaman curry paste (store any remaining paste in an airtight container in the refrigerator for up to 1 week).
   - Stir-fry the curry paste for 1-2 minutes until fragrant.
3. **Add Beef (or Protein):**
   - Add cubed beef (or protein of choice) to the pot. Cook until browned on all sides, about 5-7 minutes.
4. **Simmer with Coconut Milk:**
   - Pour in coconut milk and chicken broth (or vegetable broth). Stir to combine.
5. **Add Potatoes and Onions:**
   - Add peeled and chopped potatoes, sliced onion, roasted peanuts, torn kaffir lime leaves (if using), and cinnamon stick to the pot. Stir well.
6. **Simmer the Curry:**
   - Bring the curry to a boil, then reduce heat to low. Cover and simmer for 30-40 minutes, stirring occasionally, until the beef (or protein) is tender and potatoes are cooked through.
7. **Adjust Seasoning:**
   - Stir in tamarind paste (or lime juice), fish sauce (or soy sauce), and palm sugar (or brown sugar). Adjust seasoning to balance the flavors of sweet, sour, salty, and spicy.
8. **Serve:**
   - Remove from heat and discard the cinnamon stick. Serve hot Massaman Curry over steamed jasmine rice.
9. **Garnish and Enjoy:**
   - Garnish with chopped fresh cilantro leaves. Serve with additional lime wedges and enjoy your homemade Massaman Curry!

Tips:

- Adjust the level of spiciness by adding more or fewer dried red chilies in the curry paste.

- For a vegetarian or vegan version, substitute beef with tofu or mixed vegetables like carrots, bell peppers, and sweet potatoes.
- Use fresh ingredients like lemongrass and kaffir lime leaves for authentic flavors, or substitute with dried versions if unavailable.

This recipe captures the rich and aromatic flavors of Massaman Curry, making it a comforting and satisfying dish to enjoy with family and friends.

Som Tum (Green Papaya Salad)

Ingredients:

For the Salad:

- 1 medium green papaya (about 1 lb), peeled and julienned
- 1 cup cherry tomatoes, halved
- 2-3 Thai bird's eye chilies, chopped (adjust to taste)
- 2 cloves garlic, minced
- 2 tablespoons roasted peanuts, coarsely chopped
- 2 tablespoons dried shrimp, optional (soaked in warm water for 5 minutes and drained)
- 1-2 tablespoons fish sauce (adjust to taste)
- 1-2 tablespoons palm sugar or brown sugar (adjust to taste)
- Juice of 1-2 limes (adjust to taste)
- 2 tablespoons tamarind juice or tamarind paste dissolved in 2 tablespoons warm water
- 1 cup long beans or green beans, cut into 1-inch pieces (optional)
- 1/4 cup carrot, shredded (optional)
- 1/4 cup fresh cilantro leaves, chopped
- 1/4 cup fresh Thai basil leaves, torn (optional)
- Lime wedges, for serving

Instructions:

1. **Prepare the Green Papaya:**
   - Peel the green papaya and cut it in half lengthwise. Remove the seeds. Use a julienne peeler or a sharp knife to slice the papaya into thin matchstick-like strips. Place the julienned papaya in a large mixing bowl.
2. **Make the Dressing:**
   - In a small bowl, combine minced garlic, chopped Thai bird's eye chilies, fish sauce, palm sugar or brown sugar, lime juice, and tamarind juice (or tamarind paste dissolved in warm water). Stir well until the sugar is dissolved and flavors are combined.
3. **Assemble the Salad:**
   - Add cherry tomatoes, soaked dried shrimp (if using), and optional long beans or green beans and shredded carrot to the bowl with julienned papaya.
4. **Toss with Dressing:**
   - Pour the dressing over the salad ingredients. Use salad tongs or clean hands to toss everything together, ensuring the papaya strips are evenly coated with the dressing.
5. **Adjust Seasoning:**
   - Taste the salad and adjust seasoning as needed. Add more fish sauce for saltiness, lime juice for sourness, or sugar for sweetness according to your preference.
6. **Add Herbs and Peanuts:**

        - Add chopped roasted peanuts, fresh cilantro leaves, and torn Thai basil leaves (if using) to the salad. Gently toss to combine.
7. **Serve:**
    - Transfer the Som Tum to a serving plate or bowl. Garnish with additional peanuts and fresh herbs. Serve immediately with lime wedges on the side.

Tips:

- Adjust the spiciness of the salad by adding more or fewer Thai bird's eye chilies.
- For a vegetarian version, omit the dried shrimp or substitute with tofu or roasted cashews.
- Make sure to handle Thai bird's eye chilies carefully, as they are very spicy. Use gloves or wash hands thoroughly after handling.
- Som Tum is traditionally served as a side dish with grilled meats, sticky rice, or as part of a larger Thai meal.

Enjoy the vibrant and refreshing flavors of homemade Som Tum (Green Papaya Salad)!

Pad Krapow Moo (Thai Basil Pork)

Ingredients:

- 1 lb (450g) ground pork (or substitute with chicken, beef, or tofu)
- 4 cloves garlic, minced
- 2-3 Thai bird's eye chilies, chopped (adjust to taste)
- 1 tablespoon vegetable oil
- 1 tablespoon oyster sauce
- 1 tablespoon soy sauce
- 1 teaspoon fish sauce
- 1 teaspoon sugar
- 1 cup fresh Thai holy basil leaves (or substitute with regular basil leaves)
- Fresh Thai bird's eye chilies, sliced (optional, for extra heat)
- Fried egg, for serving (optional)
- Cooked jasmine rice, for serving

Instructions:

1. **Prepare the Ingredients:**
   - In a small bowl, mix together oyster sauce, soy sauce, fish sauce, and sugar. Set aside.
2. **Stir-Fry the Pork:**
   - Heat vegetable oil in a large wok or skillet over medium-high heat. Add minced garlic and chopped Thai bird's eye chilies. Stir-fry for about 30 seconds until fragrant.
   - Add ground pork (or protein of choice) to the wok. Break up the meat with a spatula and stir-fry until browned and cooked through, about 5-7 minutes.
3. **Add Sauce:**
   - Pour the sauce mixture over the cooked pork. Stir well to coat the meat evenly with the sauce.
4. **Add Basil Leaves:**
   - Add fresh Thai holy basil leaves (or regular basil leaves) to the wok. Stir-fry for another 1-2 minutes until the basil leaves are wilted and aromatic.
5. **Adjust Seasoning:**
   - Taste and adjust the seasoning if needed. Add more soy sauce, fish sauce, or sugar according to your preference.
6. **Serve:**
   - Remove from heat. Serve hot Pad Krapow Moo over steamed jasmine rice.
7. **Garnish (optional):**
   - Garnish with additional sliced Thai bird's eye chilies for extra heat. Serve with a fried egg on top for a traditional Thai meal experience.

Tips:

- **Thai Holy Basil:** If you can find Thai holy basil, it adds an authentic peppery and slightly spicy flavor to the dish. If not available, regular basil leaves are a good substitute.
- **Spiciness:** Adjust the spiciness of the dish by adding more or fewer Thai bird's eye chilies. Be cautious as they are very spicy.
- **Variations:** Pad Krapow can be made with different proteins such as chicken, beef, shrimp, or tofu. Adjust cooking time accordingly based on the protein used.

Enjoy making and savoring this flavorful Thai Basil Pork dish, perfect for a quick and satisfying meal with jasmine rice!

Pad See Ew (Stir-Fried Noodles)

Ingredients:

- 8 oz (225g) wide rice noodles (fresh or dried)
- 1/2 lb (225g) chicken thighs, thinly sliced (or substitute with beef, pork, shrimp, or tofu)
- 2 cloves garlic, minced
- 2 cups Chinese broccoli (Gai Lan) or broccoli florets, cut into bite-sized pieces
- 2 eggs, beaten
- 2 tablespoons vegetable oil
- 2 tablespoons soy sauce
- 1 tablespoon oyster sauce
- 1 tablespoon dark soy sauce (or substitute with regular soy sauce and a pinch of sugar for color)
- 1 tablespoon fish sauce
- 1 tablespoon sugar
- White pepper, to taste
- Lime wedges, for serving

Instructions:

1. **Prepare the Rice Noodles:**
   - If using dried rice noodles, soak them in warm water for about 30 minutes until softened. Drain well before cooking. If using fresh rice noodles, separate them gently with your fingers.
2. **Stir-Fry the Chicken (or Protein):**
   - Heat 1 tablespoon of vegetable oil in a wok or large skillet over medium-high heat. Add minced garlic and stir-fry for about 30 seconds until fragrant.
   - Add thinly sliced chicken thighs (or protein of choice) to the wok. Stir-fry until the chicken is cooked through, about 4-5 minutes. Remove from the wok and set aside.
3. **Cook the Vegetables:**
   - In the same wok, add another tablespoon of vegetable oil. Add Chinese broccoli (or broccoli florets) and stir-fry for 2-3 minutes until crisp-tender. Push the vegetables to one side of the wok.
4. **Cook the Eggs:**
   - Pour beaten eggs into the empty side of the wok. Allow them to set slightly, then scramble until fully cooked.
5. **Stir-Fry Noodles:**
   - Add the drained rice noodles to the wok. Use tongs to gently toss and stir-fry the noodles with the vegetables and eggs.
6. **Add Sauces:**

- Combine soy sauce, oyster sauce, dark soy sauce (or regular soy sauce), fish sauce, and sugar in a small bowl. Pour the sauce mixture evenly over the noodles.

7. **Combine and Season:**
   - Continue to stir-fry the noodles until they are evenly coated with the sauce and heated through. Add white pepper to taste.
8. **Add Chicken (or Protein) Back In:**
   - Return the cooked chicken (or protein) to the wok. Toss everything together until well combined and heated through.
9. **Serve:**
   - Remove from heat. Serve hot Pad See Ew immediately, garnished with lime wedges on the side.

Tips:

- **Noodles:** Wide rice noodles are traditionally used for Pad See Ew. If unavailable, you can use other types of wide rice noodles or even flat rice noodles.
- **Vegetables:** Chinese broccoli (Gai Lan) is common, but you can also use broccoli florets or other vegetables like bok choy or bell peppers.
- **Customize:** Feel free to adjust the level of sweetness (sugar), saltiness (soy sauce), or spiciness (optional chili flakes) to suit your taste preference.
- **Serve:** Pad See Ew is traditionally served with lime wedges on the side for squeezing over the noodles before eating.

Enjoy preparing and savoring this comforting and flavorful Thai stir-fried noodle dish, Pad See Ew!

Tom Kha Gai (Chicken Coconut Soup)

Ingredients:

- 1 lb (450g) chicken thighs or breast, thinly sliced
- 4 cups chicken broth (or vegetable broth)
- 1 can (14 oz) coconut milk
- 1 stalk lemongrass, cut into 2-inch pieces and smashed
- 4-5 slices galangal (or substitute with ginger)
- 4-5 kaffir lime leaves, torn into pieces
- 6-8 Thai bird's eye chilies, lightly crushed (adjust to taste)
- 3-4 cloves garlic, minced
- 1 medium onion, thinly sliced
- 1 cup mushrooms (such as straw mushrooms or button mushrooms), sliced
- 1-2 tablespoons fish sauce (adjust to taste)
- 2 tablespoons lime juice (adjust to taste)
- 1-2 tablespoons palm sugar or brown sugar (adjust to taste)
- Fresh cilantro leaves, chopped, for garnish
- Fresh Thai basil leaves, torn (optional), for garnish

Instructions:

1. **Prepare the Broth:**
   - In a large pot, bring chicken broth to a gentle boil over medium-high heat.
2. **Add Aromatics:**
   - Add smashed lemongrass pieces, galangal slices, torn kaffir lime leaves, and crushed Thai bird's eye chilies to the boiling broth. Simmer for 5-10 minutes to infuse the flavors into the broth.
3. **Cook Chicken and Vegetables:**
   - Add thinly sliced chicken thighs (or breast), minced garlic, thinly sliced onion, and sliced mushrooms to the pot. Cook until the chicken is cooked through and vegetables are tender, about 5-7 minutes.
4. **Add Coconut Milk:**
   - Pour in coconut milk, stirring well to combine with the broth and chicken mixture. Bring the soup back to a gentle simmer.
5. **Season the Soup:**
   - Stir in fish sauce, lime juice, and palm sugar (or brown sugar). Adjust the seasoning to balance the flavors of salty, sour, and sweet according to your taste preference.
6. **Simmer Further:**
   - Allow the soup to simmer gently for another 5-10 minutes to meld the flavors together.
7. **Garnish and Serve:**

- Remove from heat. Discard lemongrass pieces and galangal slices. Taste and adjust seasoning if needed.
- Ladle Tom Kha Gai into serving bowls. Garnish with chopped fresh cilantro leaves and torn Thai basil leaves (if using).

8. **Serve Hot:**
   - Serve Tom Kha Gai hot as a comforting and flavorful Thai soup. Enjoy it with steamed jasmine rice or as a starter to a Thai meal.

Tips:

- **Ingredients Substitutions:** If you can't find galangal, substitute with ginger for a similar flavor profile. Thai bird's eye chilies can be adjusted or omitted for less heat.
- **Vegetarian Version:** For a vegetarian or vegan option, substitute chicken with tofu or mixed vegetables like bell peppers, broccoli, and carrots. Use vegetable broth instead of chicken broth and soy sauce instead of fish sauce.
- **Herbs:** Fresh herbs like cilantro and Thai basil add brightness to the soup. If unavailable, use regular basil and parsley as substitutes.

Panang Curry

Ingredients:

For the Panang Curry Paste:

- 4-5 dried red chilies, soaked in warm water to soften
- 2 shallots, chopped
- 4 cloves garlic, chopped
- 1 thumb-sized piece of galangal, chopped (or substitute with ginger)
- 1 stalk lemongrass, thinly sliced (white part only)
- 1 teaspoon shrimp paste (optional, omit for vegetarian)
- 1 teaspoon ground coriander
- 1 teaspoon ground cumin
- 1/2 teaspoon ground white pepper
- 1/2 teaspoon ground nutmeg
- 1 tablespoon roasted peanuts, crushed
- Zest of 1 lime
- 1 tablespoon vegetable oil

For the Panang Curry:

- 1 lb (450g) beef (such as flank steak or sirloin), thinly sliced (or substitute with chicken, pork, or tofu)
- 1 can (14 oz) coconut milk
- 1-2 tablespoons Panang curry paste (from above, adjust to taste)
- 2-3 kaffir lime leaves, torn into pieces
- 2 tablespoons fish sauce
- 1-2 tablespoons palm sugar or brown sugar (adjust to taste)
- 1/2 cup Thai basil leaves, torn (optional)
- 1/4 cup roasted peanuts, crushed, for garnish (optional)
- Cooked jasmine rice, for serving

Instructions:

1. **Prepare the Panang Curry Paste:**
    - In a food processor or mortar and pestle, blend soaked dried red chilies, chopped shallots, chopped garlic, chopped galangal (or ginger), thinly sliced lemongrass, shrimp paste (if using), ground coriander, ground cumin, ground white pepper, ground nutmeg, crushed roasted peanuts, lime zest, and vegetable oil until a smooth paste forms. Add a little water if needed to help blend.
2. **Cook the Curry:**
    - Heat a large skillet or wok over medium-high heat. Add 1-2 tablespoons of Panang curry paste (adjust amount to your spice preference) and stir-fry for 1-2 minutes until fragrant.

3. **Add Coconut Milk:**
   - Pour in coconut milk, stirring well to combine with the curry paste. Bring to a gentle simmer.
4. **Simmer the Beef (or Protein):**
   - Add thinly sliced beef (or protein of choice) to the simmering coconut milk mixture. Cook for 5-7 minutes until the beef is cooked through and tender.
5. **Season the Curry:**
   - Stir in torn kaffir lime leaves, fish sauce, and palm sugar (or brown sugar). Taste and adjust seasoning as needed for a balance of salty, sweet, and savory flavors.
6. **Finish and Serve:**
   - Remove from heat and stir in torn Thai basil leaves (if using). The residual heat will wilt the basil leaves slightly.
7. **Garnish and Serve:**
   - Ladle Panang Curry into serving bowls. Garnish with crushed roasted peanuts (if desired) and serve hot with jasmine rice.

Tips:

- **Panang Curry Paste:** Adjust the amount of Panang curry paste according to your preferred level of spiciness and flavor intensity.
- **Meat Options:** Feel free to substitute beef with chicken, pork, shrimp, or tofu based on your dietary preferences.
- **Thai Basil:** Thai basil adds a unique flavor to Panang Curry. If unavailable, regular basil can be used as a substitute.
- **Customization:** You can add additional vegetables like bell peppers, bamboo shoots, or green beans to the curry for added texture and flavor.

Enjoy the rich and creamy flavors of homemade Panang Curry, perfect with jasmine rice for a satisfying Thai meal!

Khao Pad (Thai Fried Rice)

Ingredients:

- 3 cups cooked jasmine rice (preferably day-old rice, chilled)
- 2 tablespoons vegetable oil
- 2 cloves garlic, minced
- 1 small onion, finely chopped
- 1-2 Thai bird's eye chilies, finely chopped (adjust to taste)
- 1 cup protein of choice (e.g., chicken, shrimp, pork, tofu), diced
- 1/2 cup mixed vegetables (e.g., peas, carrots, bell peppers), diced
- 2 eggs, beaten
- 2 tablespoons soy sauce
- 1 tablespoon fish sauce (optional)
- 1 tablespoon oyster sauce
- 1 teaspoon sugar
- Freshly ground black pepper, to taste
- Spring onions (scallions), chopped, for garnish
- Fresh cilantro leaves, chopped, for garnish
- Lime wedges, for serving

Instructions:

1. **Prepare the Ingredients:**
    - Ensure all ingredients are chopped and ready before starting to cook. Have the cooked jasmine rice ready, ideally chilled or at room temperature.
2. **Stir-Fry the Aromatics:**
    - Heat vegetable oil in a large wok or skillet over medium-high heat. Add minced garlic and chopped Thai bird's eye chilies. Stir-fry for about 30 seconds until fragrant.
3. **Add Protein and Vegetables:**
    - Add diced protein (e.g., chicken, shrimp, pork, tofu) to the wok. Stir-fry until the protein is almost cooked through, about 3-4 minutes.
    - Add diced mixed vegetables (e.g., peas, carrots, bell peppers). Continue to stir-fry for another 2-3 minutes until vegetables are tender-crisp.
4. **Scramble Eggs:**
    - Push the protein and vegetables to one side of the wok. Pour beaten eggs into the empty side of the wok. Allow them to set slightly, then scramble until fully cooked.
5. **Combine with Rice:**
    - Add cooked jasmine rice to the wok. Use a spatula or wooden spoon to break up any clumps and combine with the protein, vegetables, and eggs.
6. **Season the Fried Rice:**

- Drizzle soy sauce, fish sauce (if using), and oyster sauce over the rice mixture. Sprinkle sugar and freshly ground black pepper. Stir-fry everything together until well combined and heated through.
7. **Adjust Seasoning:**
    - Taste and adjust seasoning as needed. Add more soy sauce for saltiness, fish sauce for depth of flavor, or sugar to balance the flavors.
8. **Garnish and Serve:**
    - Remove from heat. Garnish with chopped spring onions (scallions) and fresh cilantro leaves. Serve hot Khao Pad immediately with lime wedges on the side.

Tips:

- **Rice:** Day-old rice works best for Khao Pad as it is drier and less sticky, resulting in better texture when stir-fried. If using freshly cooked rice, spread it out on a tray and refrigerate for at least an hour before using.
- **Protein Options:** Feel free to use any protein of your choice or combine multiple proteins for variety.
- **Vegetables:** Use a mix of vegetables for color and texture. Frozen mixed vegetables can be a convenient option.
- **Customization:** Add extras like chopped pineapple, cashew nuts, or raisins for a unique twist to your fried rice.

Enjoy preparing and savoring this classic Thai Fried Rice, Khao Pad, which makes for a delicious and satisfying meal on its own or as part of a larger Thai feast!

Larb (Spicy Thai Salad)

Ingredients:

For the Larb:

- 1 lb (450g) ground chicken, pork, or beef (or use tofu for a vegetarian version)
- 2 tablespoons vegetable oil
- 3-4 shallots, finely chopped
- 3-4 cloves garlic, minced
- 2-3 Thai bird's eye chilies, finely chopped (adjust to taste)
- 2 tablespoons fish sauce
- Juice of 2-3 limes (adjust to taste)
- 1 tablespoon palm sugar or brown sugar (adjust to taste)
- 2-3 tablespoons toasted rice powder (see note below)
- 1/2 cup fresh cilantro leaves, chopped
- 1/2 cup fresh mint leaves, chopped
- 1/4 cup fresh Thai basil leaves, chopped (optional)
- Green leaf lettuce or cabbage leaves, for serving
- Sliced cucumber and/or Thai bird's eye chilies, for garnish (optional)

For the Toasted Rice Powder:

- 2 tablespoons uncooked sticky rice (glutinous rice)

Instructions:

1. **Prepare the Toasted Rice Powder:**
   - Heat a dry skillet over medium heat. Add uncooked sticky rice (glutinous rice) and toast, stirring frequently, until golden brown and fragrant, about 5-7 minutes.
   - Remove from heat and let cool. Transfer toasted rice to a mortar and pestle or spice grinder. Grind into a coarse powder. Set aside.
2. **Cook the Ground Meat (or Tofu):**
   - Heat vegetable oil in a large skillet or wok over medium-high heat. Add finely chopped shallots and minced garlic. Stir-fry for 1-2 minutes until fragrant.
   - Add ground meat (or crumbled tofu) to the skillet. Cook, breaking up the meat with a spatula, until browned and cooked through, about 5-7 minutes.
3. **Season the Larb:**
   - Stir in chopped Thai bird's eye chilies (adjust amount to your spice preference), fish sauce, lime juice, and palm sugar (or brown sugar). Mix well to combine and cook for another minute.
4. **Add Toasted Rice Powder:**
   - Remove the skillet from heat. Sprinkle 2-3 tablespoons of toasted rice powder over the cooked meat mixture. The toasted rice powder adds a nutty flavor and helps to thicken the sauce.

5. **Mix in Fresh Herbs:**
    - Add chopped fresh cilantro leaves, mint leaves, and Thai basil leaves (if using) to the skillet. Toss everything together until well combined.
6. **Serve Larb:**
    - Arrange green leaf lettuce or cabbage leaves on a serving platter. Spoon the Larb mixture onto the leaves.
7. **Garnish and Serve:**
    - Garnish with additional fresh herbs, sliced cucumber, and/or Thai bird's eye chilies (if desired). Serve Larb immediately as a main dish or part of a Thai meal. It's traditionally eaten with sticky rice or as a side dish with fresh vegetables.

Tips:

- **Toasted Rice Powder:** If you prefer a shortcut, you can also find pre-made toasted rice powder in some Asian grocery stores or online. It adds a unique texture and flavor to the Larb.
- **Spiciness:** Adjust the amount of Thai bird's eye chilies according to your heat preference. Be cautious as they are very spicy.
- **Vegetarian Option:** Substitute ground meat with crumbled tofu or a mix of diced mushrooms and vegetables for a vegetarian or vegan version of Larb.

Enjoy preparing and savoring this spicy and aromatic Thai salad, Larb, which is bursting with fresh flavors and textures!

Gaeng Keow Wan Gai (Thai Green Chicken Curry)

Ingredients:

For the Green Curry Paste:

- 1 cup fresh Thai basil leaves
- 1/2 cup fresh cilantro leaves and stems
- 2-3 Thai green chilies, chopped (adjust to taste)
- 1 shallot, chopped
- 3 cloves garlic, chopped
- 1 thumb-sized piece of galangal or ginger, chopped
- 1 stalk lemongrass, thinly sliced (white part only)
- 1 tablespoon coriander seeds, toasted and ground
- 1 teaspoon cumin seeds, toasted and ground
- 1/2 teaspoon white pepper
- 2 kaffir lime leaves, torn
- Zest of 1 lime
- 1 tablespoon shrimp paste (or substitute with 1 tablespoon soy sauce for vegetarian/vegan option)
- 1 tablespoon vegetable oil

For the Curry:

- 1 lb (450g) chicken thighs or breast, thinly sliced
- 1 can (14 oz) coconut milk
- 1 cup chicken broth (or vegetable broth)
- 1 cup Thai eggplant, quartered (or substitute with regular eggplant)
- 1 red bell pepper, sliced
- 1 cup bamboo shoots, sliced (optional)
- 2 tablespoons fish sauce
- 1-2 tablespoons palm sugar or brown sugar, to taste
- Fresh Thai basil leaves, torn, for garnish
- Red chili slices, for garnish (optional)
- Cooked jasmine rice, for serving

Instructions:

1. **Prepare the Green Curry Paste:**
   - In a food processor or blender, combine Thai basil leaves, cilantro leaves and stems, chopped Thai green chilies, shallot, garlic, galangal or ginger, thinly sliced lemongrass, ground coriander seeds, ground cumin seeds, white pepper, torn kaffir lime leaves, lime zest, shrimp paste (or soy sauce), and vegetable oil. Blend until a smooth paste forms. Add a little water if needed to help blend.
2. **Cook the Curry:**

- Heat a large pot or deep skillet over medium-high heat. Add 1-2 tablespoons of the prepared green curry paste (adjust amount to your spice preference). Stir-fry for 1-2 minutes until fragrant.
3. **Add Coconut Milk and Broth:**
    - Pour in coconut milk and chicken broth. Stir well to combine with the green curry paste. Bring to a gentle simmer.
4. **Simmer with Chicken:**
    - Add thinly sliced chicken thighs or breast to the simmering curry sauce. Cook for 5-7 minutes until the chicken is almost cooked through.
5. **Add Vegetables:**
    - Add Thai eggplant quarters, sliced red bell pepper, and bamboo shoots (if using) to the curry. Stir to combine and simmer for another 5-7 minutes until the vegetables are tender and the chicken is fully cooked.
6. **Season the Curry:**
    - Stir in fish sauce and palm sugar (or brown sugar) to taste. Adjust the seasoning for a balance of salty, sweet, and savory flavors.
7. **Garnish and Serve:**
    - Remove from heat. Garnish with torn fresh Thai basil leaves and red chili slices (if using). Serve hot Gaeng Keow Wan Gai immediately with cooked jasmine rice.

Tips:

- **Curry Paste:** You can adjust the spiciness of the curry paste by adding more or fewer Thai green chilies. Be cautious as they are very spicy.
- **Vegetables:** Feel free to customize the curry with your favorite vegetables such as baby corn, snow peas, or zucchini.
- **Thai Basil:** Thai basil adds a distinct flavor to the curry. If unavailable, regular basil can be used as a substitute.
- **Fish Sauce:** Use good quality fish sauce for authentic Thai flavors. Adjust the amount according to your taste preference.

Enjoy making and savoring this aromatic and creamy Thai Green Chicken Curry, perfect with jasmine rice for a comforting and satisfying meal!

Pad Pak Bung Fai Daeng (Stir-Fried Morning Glory)

Ingredients:

- 1 bunch of morning glory (water spinach), about 300-400g
- 2-3 cloves garlic, minced
- 2-3 Thai bird's eye chilies, chopped (adjust to taste)
- 1 tablespoon oyster sauce
- 1 tablespoon soy sauce
- 1 teaspoon fish sauce
- 1 teaspoon sugar
- 1/4 cup chicken broth or water
- 2 tablespoons vegetable oil
- Optional: sliced red bell pepper, sliced onion, or sliced carrots for extra vegetables

Instructions:

1. **Prepare the Morning Glory:**
   - Rinse the morning glory thoroughly under cold water. Trim off any tough stems and cut into 3-inch lengths.
2. **Prepare the Sauce Mixture:**
   - In a small bowl, mix together oyster sauce, soy sauce, fish sauce, sugar, and chicken broth (or water). Stir until the sugar is dissolved. Set aside.
3. **Stir-Fry the Morning Glory:**
   - Heat vegetable oil in a wok or large skillet over medium-high heat. Add minced garlic and chopped Thai bird's eye chilies. Stir-fry for about 30 seconds until fragrant.
4. **Add Morning Glory:**
   - Add the morning glory to the wok. Stir-fry quickly, using tongs or a spatula to toss the vegetables continuously.
5. **Add Sauce Mixture:**
   - Pour the prepared sauce mixture over the morning glory. Continue to stir-fry for 1-2 minutes until the morning glory is wilted and coated evenly with the sauce. If using additional vegetables like red bell pepper or onion, add them at this stage.
6. **Check for Doneness:**
   - Taste a piece of morning glory to check for desired doneness. It should be tender yet still crisp.
7. **Serve:**
   - Remove from heat and transfer the stir-fried morning glory to a serving dish. Serve hot as a side dish with steamed jasmine rice.

Tips:

- **Morning Glory:** If you cannot find morning glory, you can substitute with other leafy greens such as spinach or kale. Adjust cooking time accordingly as these greens may cook faster.
- **Spiciness:** Adjust the amount of Thai bird's eye chilies according to your spice preference. Be cautious as they are very spicy.
- **Vegetables:** Feel free to add sliced red bell pepper, sliced onion, or other vegetables of your choice to enhance the dish.

Enjoy making this flavorful and nutritious Thai Stir-Fried Morning Glory, perfect as a quick and delicious addition to your meal!

Pad Prik Khing (Stir-Fried Green Beans with Red Curry Paste)

Ingredients:

- 300g green beans, trimmed and cut into 2-inch pieces
- 200g protein of choice (chicken, pork, beef, shrimp, tofu), thinly sliced
- 2-3 tablespoons red curry paste (store-bought or homemade)
- 3-4 kaffir lime leaves, thinly sliced (optional)
- 1 red bell pepper, sliced (optional)
- 2 tablespoons vegetable oil
- 1 tablespoon fish sauce
- 1 tablespoon soy sauce
- 1 teaspoon sugar
- Fresh Thai basil leaves, for garnish (optional)

Instructions:

1. **Prepare the Green Beans:**
    - Rinse the green beans under cold water, trim the ends, and cut into 2-inch pieces.
2. **Stir-Fry the Protein:**
    - Heat 1 tablespoon of vegetable oil in a wok or large skillet over medium-high heat. Add the thinly sliced protein (chicken, pork, beef, shrimp, or tofu). Stir-fry until the protein is almost cooked through. Remove from the wok and set aside.
3. **Stir-Fry the Green Beans:**
    - In the same wok or skillet, add another tablespoon of vegetable oil. Add the green beans and stir-fry for 2-3 minutes until they are tender-crisp.
4. **Add Red Curry Paste:**
    - Push the green beans to the side of the wok to create a space in the center. Add 2-3 tablespoons of red curry paste to the center and stir-fry for about 1 minute until fragrant.
5. **Combine and Season:**
    - Mix the red curry paste with the green beans. Add the sliced red bell pepper (if using), kaffir lime leaves (if using), fish sauce, soy sauce, and sugar. Stir-fry for another 1-2 minutes until everything is well combined and heated through.
6. **Return Protein to the Wok:**
    - Add the cooked protein back into the wok with the green beans and curry mixture. Stir well to coat everything evenly with the sauce.
7. **Check for Seasoning:**
    - Taste and adjust the seasoning if needed. Add more fish sauce for saltiness, soy sauce for depth of flavor, or sugar to balance the flavors.
8. **Garnish and Serve:**
    - Remove from heat and transfer the Pad Prik Khing to a serving dish. Garnish with fresh Thai basil leaves (if using). Serve hot with steamed jasmine rice.

Tips:

- **Red Curry Paste:** You can use store-bought red curry paste or make your own using a blend of red chilies, garlic, shallots, lemongrass, galangal or ginger, coriander seeds, cumin seeds, and shrimp paste (or soy sauce for vegetarian/vegan option).
- **Protein Options:** Feel free to use your favorite protein or a combination of different proteins. Adjust cooking times accordingly.
- **Vegetables:** Add other vegetables like sliced red bell pepper, onion, or carrots for extra flavor and texture.

Enjoy making this flavorful and aromatic Pad Prik Khing at home! It's a wonderful dish that pairs perfectly with steamed jasmine rice for a satisfying Thai meal.

Pad Grapow Gai (Stir-Fried Chicken with Holy Basil)

Ingredients:

- 1 lb (450g) chicken thighs or breast, thinly sliced
- 2 tablespoons vegetable oil
- 4-5 cloves garlic, minced
- 2-3 Thai bird's eye chilies, finely chopped (adjust to taste)
- 1 red bell pepper, thinly sliced (optional)
- 1 onion, thinly sliced (optional)
- 2 cups fresh holy basil leaves (or Thai basil leaves)
- 2 tablespoons oyster sauce
- 1 tablespoon soy sauce
- 1 tablespoon fish sauce
- 1 teaspoon sugar
- Freshly ground black pepper, to taste
- Cooked jasmine rice, for serving

Instructions:

1. **Prepare the Chicken and Ingredients:**
   - Thinly slice the chicken thighs or breast. Prepare minced garlic, chopped Thai bird's eye chilies, red bell pepper (if using), onion (if using), and measure out fresh holy basil leaves.
2. **Stir-Fry the Chicken:**
   - Heat vegetable oil in a wok or large skillet over medium-high heat. Add minced garlic and chopped Thai bird's eye chilies. Stir-fry for about 30 seconds until fragrant.
3. **Add Chicken and Vegetables:**
   - Add thinly sliced chicken to the wok. Stir-fry until the chicken is almost cooked through, about 5-7 minutes.
4. **Combine Sauces and Seasonings:**
   - In a small bowl, mix oyster sauce, soy sauce, fish sauce, and sugar until well combined.
5. **Add Sauce Mixture:**
   - Pour the sauce mixture over the chicken. Stir-fry for another 1-2 minutes until the chicken is fully cooked and coated evenly with the sauce.
6. **Add Basil Leaves:**
   - Add fresh holy basil leaves (or Thai basil leaves) to the wok. Stir-fry for about 30 seconds until the basil leaves are wilted and fragrant.
7. **Adjust Seasoning:**
   - Taste and adjust the seasoning if needed. Add freshly ground black pepper to taste.
8. **Serve:**

- Remove from heat. Transfer Pad Grapow Gai to a serving dish. Serve hot with steamed jasmine rice.

Tips:

- **Basil Leaves:** Holy basil (also known as Thai basil) is traditionally used in this dish for its distinct aroma and flavor. If unavailable, you can use Thai basil or regular sweet basil as a substitute.
- **Spiciness:** Adjust the amount of Thai bird's eye chilies according to your spice preference. Be cautious as they are very spicy.
- **Vegetables:** Customize the dish by adding sliced red bell pepper, onion, or other vegetables of your choice for added texture and flavor.

Enjoy making and savoring this flavorful and aromatic Thai Stir-Fried Chicken with Holy Basil, Pad Grapow Gai, at home! It's a quick and satisfying dish that pairs perfectly with jasmine rice for a delicious meal.

Moo Ping (Thai Grilled Pork Skewers)

Ingredients:

For the Pork Skewers:

- 1 lb (450g) pork loin or pork shoulder, thinly sliced into strips
- 2 tablespoons soy sauce
- 2 tablespoons oyster sauce
- 1 tablespoon fish sauce
- 1 tablespoon sugar
- 1 tablespoon vegetable oil
- 1 teaspoon ground white pepper
- Bamboo skewers, soaked in water for 30 minutes

For the Dipping Sauce:

- 3 tablespoons soy sauce
- 2 tablespoons rice vinegar
- 1 tablespoon sugar
- 1-2 Thai bird's eye chilies, finely chopped (adjust to taste)
- 1 garlic clove, minced
- Fresh cilantro leaves, chopped (optional)

For Serving:

- Sticky rice (glutinous rice), cooked
- Sliced cucumber and lettuce leaves, for garnish (optional)

Instructions:

1. **Marinate the Pork:**
    - In a bowl, combine soy sauce, oyster sauce, fish sauce, sugar, vegetable oil, and ground white pepper. Mix well until the sugar is dissolved.
    - Add thinly sliced pork to the marinade. Toss to coat the pork evenly. Cover and refrigerate for at least 1 hour, or preferably overnight, to allow the flavors to meld.
2. **Prepare the Dipping Sauce:**
    - In a small bowl, mix together soy sauce, rice vinegar, sugar, finely chopped Thai bird's eye chilies, minced garlic, and chopped cilantro leaves (if using). Stir until the sugar is dissolved. Set aside.
3. **Skewer the Pork:**
    - Thread the marinated pork slices onto bamboo skewers, weaving the skewer through each piece to keep them secure.
4. **Grill the Pork Skewers:**

- Preheat a grill or grill pan over medium-high heat. Brush the grill grates with oil to prevent sticking.
- Grill the pork skewers for 3-4 minutes on each side, or until the pork is cooked through and nicely charred. Ensure the internal temperature of the pork reaches 145°F (63°C).

5. **Serve Moo Ping:**
   - Remove the grilled pork skewers from the grill. Serve hot Moo Ping immediately with sticky rice, sliced cucumber, lettuce leaves, and the prepared dipping sauce on the side.

Tips:

- **Pork Selection:** Use pork loin or pork shoulder for Moo Ping, as they are tender and flavorful when grilled.
- **Marinating Time:** Marinate the pork for at least 1 hour for optimal flavor, but longer marinating time will enhance the taste.
- **Grilling:** If using an outdoor grill, keep an eye on the pork to prevent burning. Alternatively, you can use a grill pan on the stove for indoor cooking.

Enjoy making and savoring these delicious Thai Grilled Pork Skewers, Moo Ping, for a flavorful and authentic Thai street food experience at home!

Gai Pad Med Mamuang (Stir-Fried Chicken with Cashew Nuts)

Ingredients:

- 1 lb (450g) chicken breast or thigh, sliced into thin strips
- 1/2 cup unsalted cashew nuts
- 2 tablespoons vegetable oil
- 4-5 cloves garlic, minced
- 1 small onion, sliced
- 1 red bell pepper, sliced
- 1 green bell pepper, sliced
- 1/2 cup sliced mushrooms (optional)
- 1/2 cup snow peas or snap peas, trimmed (optional)
- 3-4 Thai bird's eye chilies, chopped (adjust to taste)
- 1/4 cup chicken broth or water
- 2 tablespoons soy sauce
- 1 tablespoon oyster sauce
- 1 tablespoon fish sauce
- 1 tablespoon sugar
- Freshly ground black pepper, to taste
- Fresh cilantro leaves, for garnish (optional)
- Cooked jasmine rice, for serving

Instructions:

1. **Toast the Cashew Nuts:**
   - Heat a dry skillet over medium heat. Add the cashew nuts and toast them for 3-4 minutes, stirring frequently, until they are lightly golden and fragrant. Remove from heat and set aside.
2. **Stir-Fry the Chicken:**
   - Heat 1 tablespoon of vegetable oil in a wok or large skillet over medium-high heat. Add minced garlic and chopped Thai bird's eye chilies. Stir-fry for about 30 seconds until fragrant.
   - Add sliced chicken to the wok. Stir-fry until the chicken is cooked through and no longer pink, about 5-7 minutes. Remove the chicken from the wok and set aside.
3. **Stir-Fry the Vegetables:**
   - In the same wok or skillet, heat the remaining tablespoon of vegetable oil over medium-high heat. Add sliced onion, red bell pepper, green bell pepper, sliced mushrooms (if using), and snow peas or snap peas (if using). Stir-fry for 3-4 minutes until the vegetables are tender-crisp.
4. **Combine Chicken and Vegetables:**
   - Return the cooked chicken to the wok with the stir-fried vegetables. Mix well to combine.
5. **Prepare the Sauce:**

- In a small bowl, mix together chicken broth (or water), soy sauce, oyster sauce, fish sauce, and sugar until well combined.
6. **Add Sauce and Cashew Nuts:**
    - Pour the sauce mixture over the chicken and vegetables in the wok. Stir-fry for another 1-2 minutes until everything is heated through and coated evenly with the sauce.
    - Add the toasted cashew nuts to the wok. Stir well to combine.
7. **Check for Seasoning:**
    - Taste and adjust the seasoning if needed. Add freshly ground black pepper to taste.
8. **Serve:**
    - Remove from heat. Transfer Gai Pad Med Mamuang to a serving dish. Garnish with fresh cilantro leaves (if using). Serve hot with cooked jasmine rice.

Tips:

- **Cashew Nuts:** Toasting the cashew nuts enhances their flavor and adds a nice crunch to the dish. Be careful not to burn them while toasting.
- **Vegetables:** Feel free to customize the dish with your favorite vegetables such as broccoli, carrots, or baby corn.
- **Spiciness:** Adjust the amount of Thai bird's eye chilies according to your spice preference. Be cautious as they are very spicy.
- **Serving:** Gai Pad Med Mamuang is traditionally served with jasmine rice, but you can also enjoy it with noodles or on its own as a main dish.

Enjoy making and savoring this flavorful and satisfying Thai Stir-Fried Chicken with Cashew Nuts, Gai Pad Med Mamuang, at home! It's a delicious and versatile dish that is sure to become a favorite.

Pla Rad Prik (Fried Fish with Chili Sauce)

Ingredients:

For the Fried Fish:

- 2 whole fish (such as tilapia or snapper), cleaned and scaled
- Salt and pepper, to taste
- Cornstarch, for dusting
- Vegetable oil, for frying

For the Chili Sauce:

- 4-5 cloves garlic, minced
- 2-3 Thai bird's eye chilies, finely chopped (adjust to taste)
- 2 tablespoons fish sauce
- 2 tablespoons soy sauce
- 1 tablespoon sugar
- 1 tablespoon rice vinegar or lime juice
- 1/4 cup water
- 1 tablespoon cornstarch mixed with 2 tablespoons water (optional, for thickening)

For Garnish (optional):

- Fresh cilantro leaves, chopped
- Sliced red bell pepper
- Sliced green onions

Instructions:

1. **Prepare the Fish:**
   - Rinse the whole fish under cold water and pat dry with paper towels. Make diagonal cuts along the sides of the fish to help it cook evenly. Season the fish inside and out with salt and pepper.
2. **Fry the Fish:**
   - Heat vegetable oil in a large skillet or wok over medium-high heat until hot (about 350°F or 175°C). Dust the fish lightly with cornstarch, shaking off any excess.
   - Carefully place the fish into the hot oil, one at a time. Fry for about 5-7 minutes on each side, or until the fish is golden brown and cooked through. Remove from oil and drain on paper towels.
3. **Make the Chili Sauce:**
   - In a small saucepan, heat 1 tablespoon of vegetable oil over medium heat. Add minced garlic and chopped Thai bird's eye chilies. Stir-fry for about 30 seconds until fragrant.

- Add fish sauce, soy sauce, sugar, rice vinegar or lime juice, and water to the saucepan. Bring to a simmer.
- If desired, thicken the sauce with a cornstarch-water mixture by slowly adding it to the simmering sauce while stirring continuously until the desired consistency is reached. Remove from heat.

4. **Assemble Pla Rad Prik:**
   - Place the fried fish on a serving platter. Pour the prepared chili sauce over the fish, covering it evenly.
   - Garnish with chopped fresh cilantro leaves, sliced red bell pepper, and sliced green onions (if using).
5. **Serve:**
   - Serve Pla Rad Prik immediately with steamed jasmine rice and additional chili sauce on the side.

Tips:

- **Fish Selection:** Choose whole fish that are fresh and firm, such as tilapia or snapper. Make sure they are cleaned and scaled properly before cooking.
- **Frying Tips:** To achieve crispy fish, ensure the oil is hot enough before adding the fish. Fry each side until golden brown and crispy.
- **Chili Sauce:** Adjust the spiciness of the sauce by adding more or fewer Thai bird's eye chilies. Be cautious as they are very spicy.
- **Garnish:** Customize the dish with your favorite fresh herbs and vegetables for added color and flavor.

Enjoy making and savoring this delicious Thai dish, Pla Rad Prik, with its crispy fried fish and flavorful chili sauce! It's a wonderful combination of textures and tastes that is sure to impress.

Thai Crab Fried Rice

Ingredients:

- 2 cups cooked jasmine rice, preferably chilled (about 1 cup uncooked rice)
- 200g crab meat (fresh or canned), picked over for shells
- 2 eggs, beaten
- 2 cloves garlic, minced
- 1 small onion, finely chopped
- 1 red bell pepper, diced
- 1 green onion (scallion), chopped
- 1 tablespoon vegetable oil
- 1 tablespoon fish sauce
- 1 tablespoon soy sauce
- 1 tablespoon oyster sauce
- 1 teaspoon sugar
- 1/2 teaspoon white pepper
- Fresh cilantro leaves, chopped, for garnish
- Lime wedges, for serving

Instructions:

1. **Prepare the Ingredients:**
   - If using uncooked rice, cook jasmine rice according to package instructions and allow it to cool completely (chilling in the refrigerator for a few hours or overnight is ideal).
2. **Stir-Fry the Eggs:**
   - Heat vegetable oil in a wok or large skillet over medium-high heat. Pour beaten eggs into the wok and scramble them until they are cooked through. Remove from the wok and set aside.
3. **Stir-Fry the Aromatics:**
   - In the same wok, add minced garlic and chopped onion. Stir-fry for about 1 minute until fragrant and onions are translucent.
4. **Add Crab Meat and Vegetables:**
   - Add crab meat, diced red bell pepper, and chopped green onion (scallion) to the wok. Stir-fry for another 2-3 minutes until the crab meat is heated through and the vegetables are tender-crisp.
5. **Stir-Fry with Rice:**
   - Add chilled cooked jasmine rice to the wok. Use a spatula to break up any clumps of rice and mix well with the crab meat and vegetables.
6. **Season the Fried Rice:**
   - Drizzle fish sauce, soy sauce, oyster sauce, and sprinkle sugar and white pepper over the rice mixture. Stir-fry for 2-3 minutes, ensuring that the rice is well-coated with the seasonings.

7. **Add Scrambled Eggs:**
    - Return the scrambled eggs to the wok. Gently fold them into the fried rice mixture until evenly distributed.
8. **Adjust Seasoning:**
    - Taste the fried rice and adjust seasoning if needed. Add more fish sauce, soy sauce, or sugar according to your taste preference.
9. **Serve:**
    - Remove from heat and transfer Thai Crab Fried Rice to serving plates. Garnish with chopped fresh cilantro leaves. Serve hot with lime wedges on the side for squeezing over the rice.

Tips:

- **Crab Meat:** Use fresh lump crab meat or canned crab meat for convenience. Make sure to pick over the crab meat for any shells or cartilage.
- **Chilling Rice:** Chilling the cooked rice helps to prevent it from becoming mushy when stir-frying.
- **Customization:** Feel free to add additional vegetables such as peas, carrots, or baby corn for more texture and color.

Enjoy making and savoring this flavorful Thai Crab Fried Rice! It's a delicious and satisfying dish that can be enjoyed on its own or as part of a larger Thai meal.

Khao Soi (Northern Thai Curry Noodles)

Ingredients:

For the Khao Soi Paste:

- 4-5 dried red chilies, soaked in hot water until soft
- 4 cloves garlic
- 1 shallot, chopped
- 1 thumb-sized piece of ginger, sliced
- 1 tablespoon ground coriander
- 1 tablespoon ground cumin
- 1 teaspoon turmeric powder
- 1 tablespoon shrimp paste (optional)
- 2 tablespoons vegetable oil

For the Curry Broth:

- 2 tablespoons vegetable oil
- 2 cups coconut milk
- 4 cups chicken broth
- 2 tablespoons soy sauce
- 1 tablespoon fish sauce
- 1 tablespoon palm sugar or brown sugar
- 1 lb (450g) chicken thighs or breasts, thinly sliced
- 300g fresh egg noodles or dried egg noodles, cooked according to package instructions

Toppings and Garnishes:

- Crispy fried egg noodles or deep-fried egg noodles
- Fresh lime wedges
- Pickled mustard greens (optional)
- Chopped green onions
- Fresh cilantro leaves
- Thai chili oil (optional)

Instructions:

1. **Prepare the Khao Soi Paste:**
    - In a blender or food processor, combine soaked dried red chilies (seeds removed if less heat is desired), garlic, shallot, ginger, ground coriander, ground cumin, turmeric powder, and shrimp paste (if using). Blend until a smooth paste forms, adding a bit of water if needed to facilitate blending.
2. **Make the Curry Broth:**

- Heat 2 tablespoons of vegetable oil in a large pot over medium heat. Add the Khao Soi paste and sauté for 2-3 minutes until fragrant.
   - Pour in coconut milk and stir to combine with the paste. Bring to a simmer.
   - Add chicken broth, soy sauce, fish sauce, and palm sugar (or brown sugar). Stir well and bring to a gentle boil.
3. **Cook the Chicken:**
   - Add thinly sliced chicken thighs or breasts to the simmering broth. Cook for 8-10 minutes or until the chicken is cooked through and tender.
4. **Prepare the Noodles:**
   - Meanwhile, cook fresh egg noodles or dried egg noodles according to package instructions. Drain and set aside.
5. **Serve Khao Soi:**
   - Divide the cooked noodles among serving bowls. Ladle the hot Khao Soi curry broth and chicken over the noodles.
6. **Add Toppings and Garnishes:**
   - Top each bowl with crispy fried egg noodles or deep-fried egg noodles for crunch.
   - Garnish with fresh lime wedges, pickled mustard greens (if using), chopped green onions, and fresh cilantro leaves.
   - Optionally, drizzle with Thai chili oil for extra heat and flavor.
7. **Enjoy:**
   - Serve immediately while hot. Stir the toppings into the soup just before eating to combine all the flavors.

Tips:

- **Adjusting Spice Level:** Control the spiciness by adjusting the amount of dried red chilies used in the paste.
- **Chicken Substitution:** You can also use beef, pork, or tofu as a substitute for chicken.
- **Noodle Variations:** If fresh egg noodles are not available, dried egg noodles or even rice noodles can be used.

Enjoy preparing and savoring this authentic Northern Thai dish, Khao Soi, with its fragrant curry broth and delightful textures! It's a comforting and flavorful meal that captures the essence of Thai cuisine.

Yum Woon Sen (Thai Glass Noodle Salad)

Ingredients:

For the Salad:

- 100g dried glass noodles (bean thread noodles)
- 200g shrimp, peeled and deveined
- 1 cup cherry tomatoes, halved
- 1/2 cup cucumber, thinly sliced
- 1/2 cup red onion, thinly sliced
- 1/4 cup fresh cilantro leaves, chopped
- 1/4 cup fresh mint leaves, chopped
- 1/4 cup roasted peanuts, crushed
- 1-2 Thai bird's eye chilies, finely chopped (adjust to taste)

For the Dressing:

- 3 tablespoons fish sauce
- 2 tablespoons lime juice
- 1 tablespoon palm sugar or brown sugar
- 1 tablespoon vegetable oil
- 1 clove garlic, minced
- 1 teaspoon soy sauce
- 1 teaspoon chili paste (optional, for extra spice)

Optional Garnish:

- Fresh lettuce leaves, for serving
- Lime wedges

Instructions:

1. **Prepare the Glass Noodles:**
   - Bring a pot of water to a boil. Add dried glass noodles and cook according to package instructions (usually about 5-7 minutes), or until noodles are tender but still slightly chewy. Drain and rinse under cold water to stop cooking. Set aside.
2. **Cook the Shrimp:**
   - In a separate pot of boiling water, cook shrimp for about 2-3 minutes until they turn pink and are cooked through. Drain and rinse under cold water. Set aside.
3. **Prepare the Dressing:**
   - In a small bowl, whisk together fish sauce, lime juice, palm sugar (or brown sugar), vegetable oil, minced garlic, soy sauce, and chili paste (if using). Adjust the sweetness and sourness to your taste preference.
4. **Assemble the Salad:**

- In a large mixing bowl, combine cooked glass noodles, cooked shrimp, cherry tomatoes, cucumber, red onion, chopped cilantro leaves, chopped mint leaves, crushed roasted peanuts, and chopped Thai bird's eye chilies.

5. **Add the Dressing:**
    - Pour the dressing over the salad ingredients in the bowl. Toss gently to combine and coat everything evenly with the dressing.
6. **Serve:**
    - Arrange fresh lettuce leaves on a serving platter or individual plates. Spoon the Yum Woon Sen salad onto the lettuce leaves.
    - Garnish with lime wedges on the side.

Tips:

- **Vegetarian Option:** Substitute shrimp with tofu or add more vegetables like carrots, bell peppers, or mushrooms.
- **Make Ahead:** You can prepare the dressing and cook the noodles and shrimp ahead of time. Combine everything just before serving to keep the noodles from becoming soggy.
- **Adjust Spice Level:** Control the spiciness by adjusting the amount of Thai bird's eye chilies and chili paste used in the dressing.

Enjoy making and savoring this light and flavorful Thai Glass Noodle Salad, Yum Woon Sen, as a refreshing appetizer or main dish! It's perfect for hot weather and brings a wonderful balance of flavors and textures to the table.

Pad Ped Moo Pa (Spicy Jungle Curry with Pork)

Ingredients:

For the Jungle Curry Paste:

- 10 dried red chilies, soaked in hot water until softened
- 4 cloves garlic, peeled
- 1 shallot, peeled and roughly chopped
- 1 stalk lemongrass, tough outer layers removed and thinly sliced
- 1 thumb-sized piece of galangal, peeled and thinly sliced
- 1 thumb-sized piece of ginger, peeled and thinly sliced
- 1 tablespoon shrimp paste (belacan)
- 1 teaspoon ground coriander
- 1 teaspoon ground cumin
- 1 teaspoon ground turmeric
- 1/2 teaspoon ground white pepper
- 2 tablespoons vegetable oil

For the Curry:

- 500g pork loin or shoulder, thinly sliced
- 1 cup bamboo shoots, sliced
- 1 cup green beans, trimmed and cut into 1-inch pieces
- 1 cup Thai eggplants, quartered (or substitute with regular eggplant)
- 1 cup Thai basil leaves
- 2 cups chicken broth or water
- 3 tablespoons fish sauce
- 1 tablespoon soy sauce
- 1 tablespoon palm sugar (or brown sugar)
- Fresh Thai bird's eye chilies, thinly sliced (optional, for extra heat)
- Fresh cilantro leaves, for garnish
- Cooked jasmine rice, for serving

Instructions:

1. **Prepare the Jungle Curry Paste:**
    - In a blender or food processor, combine soaked dried red chilies, garlic, shallot, lemongrass, galangal, ginger, shrimp paste, ground coriander, ground cumin, ground turmeric, and ground white pepper.
    - Blend until you get a smooth paste. You may need to add a little water to facilitate blending.
2. **Cook the Pork:**
    - Heat vegetable oil in a large pot or wok over medium-high heat.

- Add 3-4 tablespoons of the Jungle Curry paste (adjust amount based on desired spiciness) and stir-fry for about 1-2 minutes until fragrant.
- Add the thinly sliced pork and stir-fry until the pork is browned and cooked through, about 5-7 minutes.

3. **Add Vegetables and Liquid:**
   - Add bamboo shoots, green beans, and Thai eggplants (or regular eggplant) to the pot. Stir well to combine with the pork and curry paste.
   - Pour in chicken broth (or water), fish sauce, soy sauce, and palm sugar. Stir to mix everything together.
4. **Simmer the Curry:**
   - Bring the curry to a boil, then reduce the heat to low.
   - Let it simmer uncovered for about 15-20 minutes, or until the vegetables are tender and the flavors have melded together.
5. **Finish and Serve:**
   - Taste and adjust the seasoning if needed, adding more fish sauce for saltiness, soy sauce for depth, or sugar to balance the flavors.
   - If you prefer more heat, add thinly sliced Thai bird's eye chilies.
   - Stir in Thai basil leaves and cook for another minute until wilted.
   - Remove from heat and garnish with fresh cilantro leaves.
6. **Serve Hot:**
   - Serve Pad Ped Moo Pa hot with jasmine rice on the side.

Tips:

- **Adjust Spice Level:** The amount of curry paste can be adjusted based on your preference for spiciness. Start with less if you prefer milder flavors.
- **Vegetable Variations:** Feel free to add other vegetables like bell peppers, baby corn, or zucchini based on your preferences and availability.
- **Authenticity:** Using Thai eggplants and bamboo shoots will give the dish a more authentic flavor, but you can substitute with regular eggplant and other vegetables as needed.

Enjoy preparing and savoring this delicious and spicy Jungle Curry with Pork, Pad Ped Moo Pa! It's a wonderful dish that showcases the bold flavors of Thai cuisine.

Pad Thai Jay (Vegetarian Pad Thai)

Ingredients:

For the Pad Thai Sauce:

- 3 tablespoons tamarind paste
- 3 tablespoons water
- 3 tablespoons soy sauce
- 2 tablespoons palm sugar or brown sugar
- 1 tablespoon vegetarian oyster sauce (optional, for added umami)
- 1 teaspoon sriracha sauce (adjust to taste)

For the Pad Thai:

- 200g dried rice noodles (pad Thai noodles)
- 200g firm tofu, cut into small cubes
- 2 tablespoons vegetable oil
- 2 cloves garlic, minced
- 1 shallot, thinly sliced
- 1 cup bean sprouts
- 1 cup sliced bell peppers (red and/or yellow)
- 1 cup sliced carrots
- 2 green onions (scallions), chopped
- 1/2 cup roasted peanuts, crushed
- Lime wedges, for serving
- Fresh cilantro leaves, for garnish
- Additional bean sprouts, for garnish

Instructions:

1. **Prepare the Pad Thai Sauce:**
    - In a small bowl, whisk together tamarind paste and water until dissolved.
    - Add soy sauce, palm sugar (or brown sugar), vegetarian oyster sauce (if using), and sriracha sauce. Stir well until sugar is dissolved. Set aside.
2. **Prepare the Rice Noodles:**
    - Cook rice noodles according to package instructions until they are just tender. Drain and rinse under cold water to stop cooking. Set aside.
3. **Cook the Tofu:**
    - Heat 1 tablespoon of vegetable oil in a large skillet or wok over medium-high heat.
    - Add tofu cubes and stir-fry until they are golden and crispy on all sides, about 5-7 minutes. Remove tofu from the skillet and set aside.
4. **Stir-Fry the Vegetables:**
    - In the same skillet or wok, add another tablespoon of vegetable oil.

- Add minced garlic and sliced shallot. Stir-fry for 1-2 minutes until fragrant.
5. **Assemble Pad Thai:**
    - Add cooked rice noodles to the skillet/wok with the garlic and shallot.
    - Pour the prepared Pad Thai sauce over the noodles. Toss everything together gently to coat the noodles with the sauce.
6. **Add Tofu and Vegetables:**
    - Add stir-fried tofu, bean sprouts, sliced bell peppers, sliced carrots, and chopped green onions to the skillet/wok.
    - Continue to stir-fry for another 2-3 minutes until all ingredients are heated through and well combined.
7. **Serve:**
    - Transfer Vegetarian Pad Thai to serving plates.
    - Garnish with crushed roasted peanuts, fresh cilantro leaves, additional bean sprouts, and lime wedges on the side.

Tips:

- **Customize Vegetables:** Feel free to add or substitute vegetables such as broccoli florets, snow peas, or baby corn.
- **Adjusting Sauce:** Adjust the sweetness or spiciness of the Pad Thai sauce to your taste preference by adding more sugar or sriracha sauce.
- **Protein Options:** Instead of tofu, you can use tempeh or simply increase the amount of vegetables for a lighter version.

Enjoy preparing and savoring this flavorful and satisfying Vegetarian Pad Thai! It's a perfect dish for both vegetarians and anyone looking to enjoy a delicious Thai noodle stir-fry at home.

Khao Niew Mamuang (Thai Mango Sticky Rice)

Ingredients:

For the Sticky Rice:

- 1 cup glutinous rice (also known as sweet rice or sticky rice)
- 1 cup coconut milk
- 1/2 cup sugar
- 1/2 teaspoon salt

For Serving:

- 2 ripe mangoes, peeled and sliced
- Toasted sesame seeds (optional, for garnish)

For the Coconut Sauce:

- 1 cup coconut milk
- 2 tablespoons sugar
- 1/4 teaspoon salt
- 1 teaspoon cornstarch mixed with 2 teaspoons water (optional, for thickening)

Instructions:

1. **Prepare the Sticky Rice:**
    - Rinse the glutinous rice under cold water until the water runs clear. Soak the rice in enough water to cover it for at least 1 hour or overnight.
2. **Steam the Sticky Rice:**
    - Drain the soaked rice and place it in a steamer lined with cheesecloth or a muslin cloth. Steam the rice over medium-high heat for about 20-25 minutes, or until the rice is tender and cooked through.
3. **Make the Coconut Sauce:**
    - In a small saucepan, combine coconut milk, sugar, and salt over medium heat. Stir until the sugar is dissolved and the mixture is heated through.
    - If you prefer a thicker sauce, stir in the cornstarch mixture and cook until the sauce has thickened slightly. Remove from heat and set aside.
4. **Season the Sticky Rice:**
    - In a separate saucepan, heat 1 cup of coconut milk with sugar and salt until dissolved.
5. **Assemble Khao Niew Mamuang:**
    - Arrange a mound of sticky rice on a serving plate.
    - Place mango slices alongside or on top of the sticky rice.
6. **Serve:**
    - Drizzle the warm coconut sauce over the sticky rice and mango.

- Optionally, sprinkle with toasted sesame seeds for added texture and flavor.
7. **Enjoy:**
   - Serve Khao Niew Mamuang warm or at room temperature. Enjoy the combination of sweet, creamy coconut rice with the fresh sweetness of mangoes.

Tips:

- **Choosing Mangoes:** Use ripe and fragrant mangoes such as Thai Honey or Ataulfo mangoes for the best flavor and texture.
- **Storing:** Khao Niew Mamuang is best enjoyed fresh. Store any leftovers in the refrigerator and reheat gently before serving.

This Thai Mango Sticky Rice recipe is a wonderful way to enjoy the classic flavors of Thai dessert at home. It's perfect for special occasions or any time you crave a sweet and satisfying treat!

Khao Soi Gai (Northern Thai Coconut Curry Noodle Soup with Chicken)

Ingredients:

For the Khao Soi Paste:

- 4-5 dried red chilies, soaked in hot water until softened
- 4 cloves garlic, peeled
- 1 shallot, peeled and roughly chopped
- 1 thumb-sized piece of ginger, peeled and sliced
- 1 thumb-sized piece of galangal, peeled and sliced
- 1 tablespoon ground coriander
- 1 tablespoon ground cumin
- 1 teaspoon turmeric powder
- 1 teaspoon curry powder
- 1 tablespoon shrimp paste (optional)
- 2 tablespoons vegetable oil

For the Soup:

- 1 tablespoon vegetable oil
- 2 cups coconut milk
- 4 cups chicken broth
- 500g chicken thighs or breasts, boneless and thinly sliced
- 200g fresh egg noodles or dried egg noodles, cooked according to package instructions

For Garnish and Toppings:

- Crispy fried egg noodles or deep-fried egg noodles
- Sliced red onion
- Pickled mustard greens (optional)
- Lime wedges
- Chopped fresh cilantro
- Thai chili paste or sriracha (optional, for extra spice)

Instructions:

1. **Prepare the Khao Soi Paste:**
    - In a blender or food processor, combine soaked dried red chilies, garlic, shallot, ginger, galangal, ground coriander, ground cumin, turmeric powder, curry powder, and shrimp paste (if using).
    - Blend until a smooth paste forms, adding a little water if needed to help blend. Set aside.
2. **Cook the Chicken:**
    - Heat vegetable oil in a large pot over medium heat.

- Add 3-4 tablespoons of the Khao Soi paste (adjust amount based on desired spiciness) and sauté for 1-2 minutes until fragrant.
- Add thinly sliced chicken and cook until chicken is browned and cooked through, about 5-7 minutes.

3. **Make the Soup:**
    - Pour in coconut milk and chicken broth. Stir well to combine.
    - Bring the soup to a simmer and let it cook for 10-15 minutes to allow the flavors to meld together.
4. **Prepare the Noodles:**
    - Meanwhile, cook fresh egg noodles or dried egg noodles according to package instructions. Drain and set aside.
5. **Serve Khao Soi:**
    - To serve, divide the cooked noodles among serving bowls.
    - Ladle the hot Khao Soi soup over the noodles.
6. **Add Toppings and Garnishes:**
    - Top each bowl with crispy fried egg noodles, sliced red onion, pickled mustard greens (if using), and chopped fresh cilantro.
    - Serve with lime wedges and Thai chili paste or sriracha on the side for those who prefer extra spice.
7. **Enjoy:**
    - Stir the toppings into the soup just before eating to combine all the flavors.
    - Serve Khao Soi Gai hot and enjoy the rich, creamy coconut curry broth with tender chicken and noodles.

Tips:

- **Adjust Spice Level:** Control the spiciness of the Khao Soi paste by adjusting the amount of dried red chilies used.
- **Vegetarian Option:** Substitute chicken with tofu or mixed vegetables for a vegetarian version.
- **Authenticity:** For an authentic touch, use fresh egg noodles and garnish with crispy fried egg noodles for texture.

Khao Soi Gai is a comforting and flavorful dish that captures the essence of Northern Thai cuisine. Enjoy making and savoring this delicious coconut curry noodle soup at home!

Kai Med Ma Muang (Chicken with Cashew Nuts)

Ingredients:

- 400g chicken breast or thigh, sliced into bite-sized pieces
- 1/2 cup raw cashew nuts
- 1 bell pepper, cut into strips
- 1 onion, sliced
- 2-3 green onions (scallions), chopped
- 3 cloves garlic, minced
- 1-inch piece of ginger, minced
- 1-2 red chilies, thinly sliced (adjust to taste)
- Vegetable oil, for stir-frying

For the Sauce:

- 2 tablespoons oyster sauce
- 1 tablespoon soy sauce
- 1 tablespoon fish sauce
- 1 tablespoon sugar
- 1/2 cup chicken broth or water
- 1 teaspoon cornstarch mixed with 2 tablespoons water (optional, for thickening)

Optional Garnish:

- Fresh cilantro leaves
- Lime wedges

Instructions:

1. **Prepare the Sauce:**
   - In a small bowl, mix together oyster sauce, soy sauce, fish sauce, sugar, and chicken broth (or water). Set aside. If you prefer a thicker sauce, mix cornstarch with water in a separate bowl and set aside.
2. **Stir-Fry the Chicken and Cashew Nuts:**
   - Heat a tablespoon of vegetable oil in a large skillet or wok over medium-high heat.
   - Add minced garlic and ginger, and stir-fry for about 30 seconds until fragrant.
   - Add sliced chicken to the skillet and stir-fry until chicken is cooked through and lightly browned, about 5-7 minutes.
3. **Add Vegetables and Sauce:**
   - Push the chicken to one side of the skillet. Add another tablespoon of vegetable oil if needed, then add cashew nuts, bell pepper strips, sliced onion, and red chilies. Stir-fry for 2-3 minutes until vegetables are tender-crisp.
4. **Combine and Thicken Sauce:**

- Pour the prepared sauce over the chicken and vegetables in the skillet. Stir everything together to coat evenly.
- If using cornstarch mixture for thickening, pour it into the skillet and stir well until the sauce thickens slightly.

5. **Finish and Serve:**
   - Remove from heat and stir in chopped green onions (scallions).
   - Transfer Kai Med Ma Muang to a serving dish.
   - Garnish with fresh cilantro leaves and serve hot with lime wedges on the side.

Tips:

- **Variations:** You can customize this dish by adding other vegetables such as broccoli, carrots, or snap peas.
- **Spice Level:** Adjust the amount of red chilies according to your preference for spiciness.
- **Serve With:** Kai Med Ma Muang is traditionally served with steamed jasmine rice, but you can also enjoy it with noodles or on its own as a main dish.

Enjoy preparing and savoring this delicious Thai Chicken with Cashew Nuts, Kai Med Ma Muang, at home! It's a flavorful and satisfying dish that's perfect for any occasion.

Pad Preaw Wan Gai (Sweet and Sour Chicken)

Ingredients:

- 400g chicken breast or thigh, thinly sliced
- 1 red bell pepper, cut into chunks
- 1 green bell pepper, cut into chunks
- 1 onion, cut into chunks
- 1 cucumber, sliced (optional)
- 1 tomato, cut into wedges
- 2-3 cloves garlic, minced
- 1 thumb-sized piece of ginger, minced
- 2-3 red or green chilies, thinly sliced (adjust to taste)
- Vegetable oil, for stir-frying

For the Sweet and Sour Sauce:

- 1/4 cup ketchup
- 3 tablespoons rice vinegar or white vinegar
- 2 tablespoons soy sauce
- 2 tablespoons sugar
- 1/2 cup pineapple juice (from canned pineapple chunks)
- 1 tablespoon cornstarch mixed with 2 tablespoons water (optional, for thickening)

Optional Garnish:

- Pineapple chunks (fresh or canned)
- Fresh cilantro leaves
- Cooked jasmine rice, for serving

Instructions:

1. **Prepare the Sweet and Sour Sauce:**
    - In a small bowl, whisk together ketchup, rice vinegar (or white vinegar), soy sauce, sugar, and pineapple juice until well combined. Set aside. If you prefer a thicker sauce, mix cornstarch with water in a separate bowl and set aside.
2. **Stir-Fry the Chicken:**
    - Heat a tablespoon of vegetable oil in a large skillet or wok over medium-high heat.
    - Add minced garlic and ginger, and stir-fry for about 30 seconds until fragrant.
    - Add sliced chicken to the skillet and stir-fry until chicken is cooked through and lightly browned, about 5-7 minutes.
3. **Add Vegetables:**

- Push the chicken to one side of the skillet. Add another tablespoon of vegetable oil if needed, then add bell pepper chunks, onion chunks, and sliced chilies. Stir-fry for 2-3 minutes until vegetables are tender-crisp.

4. **Combine with Sweet and Sour Sauce:**
    - Pour the prepared sweet and sour sauce over the chicken and vegetables in the skillet. Stir everything together to coat evenly.
    - If using cornstarch mixture for thickening, pour it into the skillet and stir well until the sauce thickens slightly.

5. **Finish and Serve:**
    - Add pineapple chunks (if using) and tomato wedges to the skillet, stirring gently to combine.
    - Remove from heat and transfer Pad Preaw Wan Gai to a serving dish.
    - Garnish with fresh cilantro leaves.
    - Serve hot with cooked jasmine rice.

Tips:

- **Vegetable Variations:** Feel free to add other vegetables such as carrots, snap peas, or broccoli florets.
- **Adjusting Sweetness:** Adjust the amount of sugar in the sauce to your taste preference for a sweeter or less sweet dish.
- **Spice Level:** Control the spiciness by adjusting the amount of chilies added or by using mild or spicy ketchup.

Enjoy preparing and savoring this flavorful Thai Sweet and Sour Chicken, Pad Preaw Wan Gai, at home! It's a vibrant and satisfying dish that pairs wonderfully with jasmine rice.

Gaeng Panang Neua (Panang Beef Curry)

Ingredients:

For the Panang Curry Paste:

- 4-5 dried red chilies, soaked in hot water until softened
- 3 cloves garlic, peeled
- 1 shallot, peeled and roughly chopped
- 1 thumb-sized piece of galangal, peeled and thinly sliced
- 1 thumb-sized piece of ginger, peeled and thinly sliced
- 1 stalk lemongrass, tough outer layers removed and thinly sliced
- 1 teaspoon ground coriander
- 1 teaspoon ground cumin
- 1/2 teaspoon ground white pepper
- 1 tablespoon shrimp paste (belacan)
- 1 tablespoon vegetable oil

For the Curry:

- 500g beef (such as sirloin or flank), thinly sliced
- 1 can (400ml) coconut milk
- 2-3 kaffir lime leaves, torn
- 1-2 tablespoons Panang curry paste (adjust to taste)
- 1 tablespoon fish sauce
- 1 tablespoon palm sugar or brown sugar
- 1/2 cup chicken broth or water
- Thai basil leaves, for garnish
- Red chili slices, for garnish (optional)

Optional Ingredients:

- 1 red bell pepper, sliced
- 1 cup bamboo shoots, sliced

Instructions:

1. **Prepare the Panang Curry Paste:**
   - In a blender or food processor, combine soaked dried red chilies, garlic, shallot, galangal, ginger, lemongrass, ground coriander, ground cumin, ground white pepper, shrimp paste, and vegetable oil.
   - Blend until smooth, adding a little water if needed to help blend. Set aside.
2. **Cook the Beef:**
   - Heat a large skillet or wok over medium-high heat.
   - Add a tablespoon of vegetable oil and swirl to coat the pan.

- Add the thinly sliced beef and stir-fry until browned on all sides, about 3-4 minutes. Remove the beef from the skillet and set aside.
3. **Simmer the Curry:**
   - In the same skillet or wok, add another tablespoon of vegetable oil if needed.
   - Add 1-2 tablespoons of Panang curry paste (adjust amount based on desired spiciness) and stir-fry for 1-2 minutes until fragrant.
   - Pour in half of the coconut milk (reserve the rest for later), stirring to incorporate with the curry paste.
4. **Add Remaining Ingredients:**
   - Add torn kaffir lime leaves, fish sauce, palm sugar (or brown sugar), and chicken broth (or water) to the skillet. Stir well to combine.
   - Bring the mixture to a simmer and let it cook for about 5 minutes to allow the flavors to meld together and the sauce to thicken slightly.
5. **Finish the Dish:**
   - Add the cooked beef back into the skillet and stir to coat with the curry sauce.
   - If using optional ingredients like red bell pepper or bamboo shoots, add them now and simmer for an additional 2-3 minutes until vegetables are tender-crisp.
6. **Serve:**
   - Remove from heat and garnish with Thai basil leaves and red chili slices (if using).
   - Serve Gaeng Panang Neua hot with steamed jasmine rice or Thai rice noodles.

Tips:

- **Adjusting Spice Level:** The spiciness of the curry can be adjusted by varying the amount of Panang curry paste and red chilies used.
- **Vegetable Variations:** Feel free to add other vegetables such as Thai eggplants, green beans, or zucchini to enhance the dish.
- **Storing:** Gaeng Panang Neua can be stored in an airtight container in the refrigerator for up to 3 days. Reheat gently before serving.

Enjoy preparing and savoring this flavorful and aromatic Panang Beef Curry, Gaeng Panang Neua, which highlights the rich and complex flavors of Thai cuisine!

Pla Kapong Neung Manao (Steamed Fish with Lime)

Ingredients:

- 1 whole white fish (such as sea bass or snapper), cleaned and scaled (about 600-800g)
- 2-3 stalks lemongrass, bruised and cut into 2-inch pieces
- 3-4 kaffir lime leaves, torn
- 1 thumb-sized piece of ginger, thinly sliced
- 3-4 cloves garlic, crushed
- 2-3 red or green chilies, sliced (adjust to taste)
- 1/4 cup fresh cilantro leaves, chopped
- 1/4 cup fresh mint leaves, chopped

For the Lime Dressing:

- 3-4 tablespoons lime juice (about 2-3 limes)
- 2 tablespoons fish sauce
- 1 tablespoon sugar
- 1 tablespoon soy sauce
- 1 tablespoon vegetable oil

Instructions:

1. **Prepare the Fish:**
    - Clean and scale the whole fish, ensuring it is gutted and cleaned thoroughly. Pat dry with paper towels.
2. **Prepare the Steaming Setup:**
    - Set up a steamer large enough to fit the whole fish. If you don't have a steamer, you can improvise one using a large pot with a rack or a colander placed over boiling water.
3. **Assemble the Steaming Ingredients:**
    - Line the steamer basket or plate with lemongrass stalks and kaffir lime leaves.
    - Place the whole fish on top of the lemongrass and lime leaves.
4. **Steam the Fish:**
    - Cover the steamer and steam the fish over medium-high heat for about 10-15 minutes, depending on the size of the fish, until it is cooked through and flakes easily with a fork. The cooking time will vary based on the thickness of the fish.
5. **Prepare the Lime Dressing:**
    - While the fish is steaming, prepare the lime dressing. In a small bowl, whisk together lime juice, fish sauce, sugar, soy sauce, and vegetable oil until well combined. Adjust the seasoning to taste, adding more lime juice or sugar if desired.
6. **Assemble and Serve:**
    - Once the fish is cooked, carefully remove it from the steamer and place it on a serving platter.

- Sprinkle crushed garlic, sliced chilies, chopped cilantro, and chopped mint over the steamed fish.
- Drizzle the lime dressing generously over the fish.

7. **Garnish and Enjoy:**
   - Garnish with additional fresh cilantro leaves and mint leaves for added freshness.
   - Serve Pla Kapong Neung Manao immediately with steamed jasmine rice and enjoy the delicate flavors of steamed fish with zesty lime dressing.

Tips:

- **Choosing the Fish:** Select a fresh whole fish with clear eyes and firm flesh for the best flavor and texture.
- **Steaming Time:** Adjust steaming time based on the size and thickness of the fish to ensure it is cooked through but still moist and tender.
- **Variations:** You can add sliced lemongrass, chopped shallots, or even a few slices of fresh ginger to enhance the aromatic flavors of the dish.

Pla Kapong Neung Manao is a light and flavorful Thai dish that highlights the natural sweetness of the fish with the tangy and aromatic lime dressing. It's perfect for a healthy and satisfying meal at home!

Pla Tod Rad Prik (Fried Fish with Chili Sauce)

Ingredients:

For the Fried Fish:

- 2 whole fish (such as tilapia or sea bass), cleaned and scaled
- Salt and pepper, to taste
- Cornstarch, for coating
- Vegetable oil, for frying

For the Chili Sauce:

- 4-5 cloves garlic, minced
- 2-3 red or green chilies, thinly sliced (adjust to taste)
- 2 tablespoons fish sauce
- 2 tablespoons soy sauce
- 1 tablespoon oyster sauce
- 1 tablespoon sugar
- 1/4 cup water
- 1 tablespoon vegetable oil

Optional Garnish:

- Sliced red chilies
- Fresh cilantro leaves

Instructions:

1. **Prepare the Fish:**
   - Clean and pat dry the whole fish. Score the fish on both sides with diagonal cuts to help it cook evenly. Season with salt and pepper.
2. **Coat and Fry the Fish:**
   - Heat vegetable oil in a large skillet or deep fryer over medium-high heat.
   - Coat the fish lightly with cornstarch, shaking off any excess.
   - Carefully place the fish in the hot oil and fry until golden brown and crispy on both sides, about 5-7 minutes per side depending on the size of the fish. Drain on paper towels to remove excess oil.
3. **Prepare the Chili Sauce:**
   - In a separate pan or skillet, heat 1 tablespoon of vegetable oil over medium heat.
   - Add minced garlic and sliced chilies, and stir-fry for about 1-2 minutes until fragrant.
4. **Make the Sauce:**
   - Add fish sauce, soy sauce, oyster sauce, sugar, and water to the skillet with garlic and chilies. Stir well to combine.

- Let the sauce simmer for 2-3 minutes until slightly thickened.
5. **Assemble and Serve:**
    - Place the fried fish on a serving platter.
    - Pour the chili sauce over the fried fish, covering it evenly.
    - Garnish with sliced red chilies and fresh cilantro leaves, if desired.
6. **Enjoy:**
    - Serve Pla Tod Rad Prik hot with steamed jasmine rice or as part of a Thai meal.

Tips:

- **Choosing the Fish:** Use fresh whole fish with firm flesh for the best results. Tilapia, sea bass, or snapper are commonly used in this dish.
- **Adjusting Spice Level:** Control the spiciness of the dish by adjusting the amount of chili peppers used.
- **Variations:** You can add additional ingredients to the chili sauce such as sliced bell peppers, onions, or basil for added flavor and texture.

Pla Tod Rad Prik is a flavorful Thai dish that combines crispy fried fish with a tangy and savory chili sauce. It's a delightful choice for a seafood lover looking to enjoy authentic Thai flavors at home!

Gai Yang (Thai Grilled Chicken)

Ingredients:

For the Marinade:

- 4 boneless, skinless chicken thighs or breasts
- 3 cloves garlic, minced
- 2 shallots, minced
- 1 stalk lemongrass, white part only, minced
- 1 thumb-sized piece of galangal or ginger, grated
- 1 tablespoon cilantro stems, finely chopped
- 2 tablespoons fish sauce
- 1 tablespoon soy sauce
- 1 tablespoon oyster sauce
- 1 tablespoon brown sugar
- 1 tablespoon vegetable oil
- 1/2 teaspoon ground turmeric
- 1/2 teaspoon ground white pepper

For the Dipping Sauce:

- 2 tablespoons fish sauce
- 2 tablespoons lime juice
- 1 tablespoon water
- 1-2 teaspoons sugar
- 1-2 red or green bird's eye chilies, finely chopped (optional)

Optional Garnish:

- Fresh cilantro leaves
- Lime wedges

Instructions:

1. **Prepare the Marinade:**
    - In a bowl, combine minced garlic, minced shallots, minced lemongrass, grated galangal or ginger, chopped cilantro stems, fish sauce, soy sauce, oyster sauce, brown sugar, vegetable oil, ground turmeric, and ground white pepper. Mix well.
2. **Marinate the Chicken:**
    - Place the chicken thighs or breasts in a shallow dish or resealable plastic bag.
    - Pour the marinade over the chicken, making sure it is evenly coated. Massage the marinade into the chicken.
    - Cover the dish or seal the bag and refrigerate for at least 2 hours, or ideally overnight, to allow the flavors to penetrate the meat.

3. **Grill the Chicken:**
    - Preheat a grill or grill pan over medium-high heat.
    - Remove the chicken from the marinade and shake off any excess.
    - Grill the chicken for 4-5 minutes per side, or until cooked through and nicely charred, with grill marks on both sides. Cooking time will vary depending on the thickness of the chicken.
4. **Make the Dipping Sauce:**
    - While the chicken is grilling, prepare the dipping sauce. In a small bowl, whisk together fish sauce, lime juice, water, and sugar until the sugar is dissolved.
    - Add chopped bird's eye chilies if you prefer extra heat.
5. **Serve:**
    - Transfer the grilled Gai Yang to a serving platter.
    - Garnish with fresh cilantro leaves and lime wedges.
    - Serve hot with the dipping sauce on the side and steamed jasmine rice or sticky rice.

Tips:

- **Grilling Tips:** Ensure the grill is properly preheated before adding the chicken to achieve nice grill marks and even cooking.
- **Marinade Flavor:** For more intense flavor, prick the chicken with a fork before marinating to allow the marinade to penetrate deeper.
- **Alternative Cooking Methods:** If you don't have a grill, you can also bake the marinated chicken in the oven or cook it in a grill pan on the stove.

Enjoy making and savoring this delicious Thai Grilled Chicken, Gai Yang, which is perfect for a summer barbecue or any time you crave authentic Thai flavors!

Kao Pad Tom Yum Goong (Tom Yum Fried Rice with Shrimp)

Ingredients:

- 2 cups cooked jasmine rice, cooled (day-old rice works best)
- 200g shrimp, peeled and deveined
- 2-3 cloves garlic, minced
- 1-2 red or green chilies, finely chopped (adjust to taste)
- 1 small onion, finely chopped
- 1/2 cup mixed vegetables (such as bell peppers, peas, carrots)
- 2-3 kaffir lime leaves, thinly sliced (optional)
- 2-3 tablespoons Tom Yum paste
- 1 tablespoon fish sauce
- 1 tablespoon soy sauce
- 1 tablespoon oyster sauce
- 1 tablespoon vegetable oil
- 1 tablespoon lime juice
- 1 tablespoon sugar
- Fresh cilantro leaves, for garnish
- Lime wedges, for serving

Instructions:

1. **Prepare the Shrimp:**
   - Heat a tablespoon of vegetable oil in a large skillet or wok over medium-high heat.
   - Add minced garlic and chopped chilies, and stir-fry for about 30 seconds until fragrant.
   - Add shrimp to the skillet and cook until they turn pink and opaque, about 2-3 minutes. Remove from the skillet and set aside.
2. **Stir-Fry the Vegetables:**
   - In the same skillet, add another tablespoon of vegetable oil if needed.
   - Add chopped onion and mixed vegetables (bell peppers, peas, carrots), and stir-fry for 2-3 minutes until vegetables are tender-crisp.
3. **Make the Tom Yum Sauce:**
   - Push the vegetables to one side of the skillet. Add Tom Yum paste to the skillet and stir-fry for about 1 minute until aromatic.
   - Mix the Tom Yum paste with the vegetables. Then, add fish sauce, soy sauce, oyster sauce, lime juice, and sugar. Stir well to combine.
4. **Add Rice and Shrimp:**
   - Add cooked jasmine rice to the skillet, breaking up any clumps with a spatula.
   - Return the cooked shrimp to the skillet.
   - Stir-fry everything together until the rice is well-coated with the sauce and heated through, about 3-4 minutes.

5. **Finish and Serve:**
    - Remove from heat and stir in thinly sliced kaffir lime leaves (if using).
    - Garnish with fresh cilantro leaves.
    - Serve hot with lime wedges on the side.

Tips:

- **Tom Yum Paste:** Adjust the amount of Tom Yum paste based on your spice preference and the intensity of flavor you desire.
- **Rice:** It's best to use cooled, day-old rice as it fries up better and is less likely to become mushy.
- **Variations:** You can add additional ingredients such as mushrooms, baby corn, or tofu to make it more hearty or vegetarian.

Enjoy preparing and savoring this delicious Tom Yum Fried Rice with Shrimp, Kao Pad Tom Yum Goong, which brings together the tangy and spicy flavors of Tom Yum soup in a comforting fried rice dish!

Pad Khing Sod Gai (Stir-Fried Chicken with Ginger)

Ingredients:

- 400g chicken breast or thigh, thinly sliced
- 2 tablespoons vegetable oil
- 2-3 cloves garlic, minced
- 1-2 red or green chilies, sliced (adjust to taste)
- 1 thumb-sized piece of ginger, thinly sliced or julienned
- 1 onion, thinly sliced
- 1 bell pepper (any color), thinly sliced
- 1-2 tablespoons soy sauce
- 1 tablespoon oyster sauce
- 1 tablespoon fish sauce
- 1 teaspoon sugar
- 1/4 cup chicken broth or water
- Fresh cilantro leaves, for garnish

Instructions:

1. **Stir-Fry the Chicken:**
   - Heat vegetable oil in a large skillet or wok over medium-high heat.
   - Add minced garlic and sliced chilies. Stir-fry for about 30 seconds until fragrant.
2. **Add Chicken and Ginger:**
   - Add thinly sliced chicken to the skillet. Stir-fry until the chicken is cooked through and lightly browned, about 5-7 minutes.
3. **Add Vegetables:**
   - Push the chicken to one side of the skillet. Add sliced ginger, onion, and bell pepper. Stir-fry for 2-3 minutes until vegetables are tender-crisp.
4. **Make the Sauce:**
   - In a small bowl, mix together soy sauce, oyster sauce, fish sauce, sugar, and chicken broth (or water).
   - Pour the sauce mixture over the chicken and vegetables in the skillet. Stir well to combine and coat everything evenly.
5. **Simmer and Serve:**
   - Let the dish simmer for another 1-2 minutes to allow the flavors to meld together and the sauce to thicken slightly.
   - Remove from heat and garnish with fresh cilantro leaves.
6. **Serve:**
   - Serve Pad Khing Sod Gai hot with steamed jasmine rice or rice noodles.

Tips:

- **Ginger:** Adjust the amount of ginger to your taste preference. More ginger will give the dish a stronger ginger flavor.
- **Vegetables:** Feel free to add other vegetables such as carrots, broccoli, or mushrooms for additional texture and flavor.
- **Spice Level:** Control the spiciness by adjusting the amount of chilies used or by using mild or spicy varieties.

Enjoy preparing and savoring this flavorful Stir-Fried Chicken with Ginger, Pad Khing Sod Gai, which is perfect for a quick and delicious Thai-inspired meal at home!

Tom Klong Pla Kra Phong (Thai Spicy Sour Sea Bass Soup)

Ingredients:

- 1 whole sea bass (about 600-800g), cleaned and scaled
- 4-5 cups water or fish stock
- 2-3 kaffir lime leaves, torn
- 1 stalk lemongrass, bruised and cut into 2-inch pieces
- 3-4 slices galangal
- 3-4 shallots, thinly sliced
- 2-3 bird's eye chilies, lightly crushed (adjust to taste)
- 3-4 tablespoons fish sauce
- 1-2 tablespoons tamarind paste
- 1-2 tablespoons palm sugar or brown sugar
- 1 tomato, cut into wedges
- Handful of straw mushrooms or other mushrooms
- Handful of Thai basil leaves
- Handful of cilantro leaves, chopped
- Lime juice, to taste

Instructions:

1. **Prepare the Sea Bass:**
   - Clean the sea bass thoroughly, removing any scales and innards. Pat dry with paper towels. Score the fish on both sides with diagonal cuts to help it cook evenly.
2. **Make the Soup Base:**
   - In a large pot, bring water or fish stock to a boil over medium-high heat.
   - Add torn kaffir lime leaves, bruised lemongrass, galangal slices, and thinly sliced shallots to the pot. Simmer for 5-10 minutes to infuse the flavors into the broth.
3. **Add Seasonings:**
   - Stir in fish sauce, tamarind paste, and palm sugar (or brown sugar) to the broth. Adjust the seasoning to achieve a balanced sweet, sour, and salty taste. Start with smaller amounts and adjust to your preference.
4. **Simmer the Sea Bass:**
   - Carefully add the sea bass to the simmering broth. Cook for about 5-7 minutes, or until the fish is cooked through and flakes easily with a fork.
5. **Add Vegetables:**
   - Add tomato wedges and mushrooms to the pot. Continue to simmer for another 2-3 minutes until the vegetables are tender.
6. **Finish and Serve:**
   - Remove the pot from heat.
   - Stir in Thai basil leaves and chopped cilantro leaves.

- Squeeze fresh lime juice into the soup, adjusting to your preferred level of tanginess.

7. **Serve:**
    - Ladle the hot and aromatic Tom Klong Pla Kra Phong into serving bowls.
    - Garnish with additional cilantro leaves and sliced bird's eye chilies for extra spice, if desired.
    - Serve immediately with steamed jasmine rice or enjoy as a soup course in a Thai meal.

Tips:

- **Fish Selection:** If sea bass (Pla Kra Phong) is not available, you can use other firm-fleshed fish such as snapper or tilapia.
- **Adjusting Spice Level:** Control the spiciness by adjusting the amount of bird's eye chilies used.
- **Vegetables:** Feel free to add other vegetables such as baby corn, bamboo shoots, or bell peppers for added texture and flavor.

Tom Klong Pla Kra Phong is a comforting and flavorful Thai soup that combines the aromatic blend of herbs and spices with the delicate sweetness of sea bass. Enjoy preparing and sharing this traditional Thai dish with friends and family!

Pad Ped Pla Dook (Spicy Catfish Stir-Fry)

Ingredients:

- 500g catfish fillets, cut into bite-sized pieces
- 2 tablespoons red curry paste
- 1 tablespoon vegetable oil
- 2-3 kaffir lime leaves, thinly sliced (optional)
- 1 red bell pepper, thinly sliced
- 1 onion, thinly sliced
- 1 tablespoon fish sauce
- 1 tablespoon soy sauce
- 1 tablespoon oyster sauce
- 1 tablespoon sugar
- 1/2 cup coconut milk
- Thai basil leaves, for garnish
- Fresh cilantro leaves, for garnish

Instructions:

1. **Prepare the Catfish:**
   - Cut the catfish fillets into bite-sized pieces. Pat dry with paper towels.
2. **Stir-Fry:**
   - Heat vegetable oil in a large skillet or wok over medium-high heat.
   - Add red curry paste to the skillet and stir-fry for about 1 minute until fragrant.
3. **Cook the Catfish:**
   - Add catfish pieces to the skillet. Stir-fry for 2-3 minutes until the catfish is lightly browned.
4. **Add Vegetables:**
   - Add thinly sliced kaffir lime leaves (if using), red bell pepper, and onion to the skillet. Stir-fry for another 2-3 minutes until the vegetables are tender-crisp.
5. **Make the Sauce:**
   - In a small bowl, mix together fish sauce, soy sauce, oyster sauce, and sugar.
   - Pour the sauce mixture into the skillet, stirring to coat the catfish and vegetables evenly.
6. **Simmer:**
   - Reduce heat to medium-low. Pour in coconut milk and stir well.
   - Let the dish simmer for 3-4 minutes, allowing the flavors to blend and the sauce to thicken slightly.
7. **Finish and Serve:**
   - Remove from heat.
   - Garnish with Thai basil leaves and fresh cilantro leaves.
8. **Serve:**
   - Serve hot with steamed jasmine rice or rice noodles.

Tips:

- **Catfish:** Use fresh catfish fillets for the best flavor and texture.
- **Spice Level:** Adjust the amount of red curry paste and bird's eye chilies according to your spice preference.
- **Vegetables:** Feel free to add other vegetables such as bamboo shoots, baby corn, or eggplant for additional texture and flavor.

Enjoy preparing and savoring this spicy and aromatic Thai dish, Pad Ped Pla Dook, which combines the richness of catfish with the vibrant flavors of Thai herbs and spices!

Gaeng Som (Thai Sour Curry)

Ingredients:

- 300g shrimp, peeled and deveined
- 2-3 tablespoons Gaeng Som paste (available at Asian grocery stores)
- 2 cups water or fish stock
- 1 cup mixed vegetables (such as pumpkin, bamboo shoots, green beans, eggplant), cut into bite-sized pieces
- 2-3 kaffir lime leaves, torn
- 1-2 tablespoons fish sauce
- 1-2 tablespoons tamarind paste
- 1 tablespoon palm sugar or brown sugar
- Thai basil leaves, for garnish
- Fresh cilantro leaves, for garnish

For Gaeng Som Paste (if making from scratch):

- 5-6 dried red chilies, soaked in water until softened
- 1 tablespoon shrimp paste (kapi)
- 1 tablespoon chopped galangal
- 1 tablespoon chopped lemongrass
- 1 tablespoon chopped shallots
- 1 tablespoon chopped garlic
- 1 teaspoon ground turmeric
- 1 teaspoon ground coriander seeds
- 1 teaspoon shrimp paste (kapi)
- 1/2 teaspoon ground white pepper

Instructions:

1. **Prepare Gaeng Som Paste (if making from scratch):**
   - In a blender or food processor, blend together soaked dried red chilies, shrimp paste (kapi), chopped galangal, lemongrass, shallots, garlic, ground turmeric, ground coriander seeds, shrimp paste (kapi), and ground white pepper until a smooth paste forms.
2. **Cooking Gaeng Som:**
   - Heat a large pot or wok over medium heat. Add 2-3 tablespoons of Gaeng Som paste and stir-fry for 1-2 minutes until fragrant.
   - Add water or fish stock to the pot and bring to a simmer.
   - Add mixed vegetables (pumpkin, bamboo shoots, green beans, eggplant) to the pot. Simmer for 5-7 minutes until vegetables are tender.

- Stir in torn kaffir lime leaves, fish sauce, tamarind paste, and palm sugar (or brown sugar). Adjust the seasoning to taste, balancing the sourness, saltiness, and sweetness.
- Add peeled and deveined shrimp to the pot. Cook for 3-5 minutes until shrimp are pink and cooked through.
3. **Finish and Serve:**
   - Remove from heat. Taste and adjust the seasoning if needed.
   - Garnish with Thai basil leaves and fresh cilantro leaves.
4. **Serve:**
   - Serve hot Gaeng Som with steamed jasmine rice.

Tips:

- **Gaeng Som Paste:** If you're short on time, you can use pre-made Gaeng Som paste available at Asian grocery stores. Adjust the amount used according to your spice preference.
- **Vegetables:** Feel free to customize the vegetables based on what you have available or prefer. Thai eggplant, pumpkin, green beans, and bamboo shoots are traditional choices.
- **Shrimp:** You can substitute shrimp with firm fish fillets such as tilapia or snapper.

Gaeng Som is a refreshing and flavorful Thai curry that balances sour, spicy, and savory flavors. It's a perfect dish to enjoy on its own with rice or as part of a larger Thai meal.

Kaeng Khiao Wan Kai (Thai Green Chicken Curry)

Ingredients:

For the Green Curry Paste:

- 3-4 green Thai chilies, chopped (adjust to taste)
- 2 shallots, chopped
- 4 cloves garlic, chopped
- 1 stalk lemongrass, white part only, chopped
- 1 thumb-sized piece of galangal or ginger, chopped
- 1 tablespoon chopped cilantro stems
- 1 tablespoon shrimp paste (kapi)
- 1 teaspoon ground coriander
- 1 teaspoon ground cumin
- 1/2 teaspoon ground white pepper
- Zest of 1 kaffir lime (optional)
- 1 tablespoon vegetable oil

For the Curry:

- 500g chicken breast or thigh, cut into bite-sized pieces
- 2-3 tablespoons green curry paste (adjust to taste)
- 1 can (14 oz) coconut milk
- 1 cup chicken broth or water
- 1 tablespoon fish sauce
- 1 tablespoon palm sugar or brown sugar
- 1 cup Thai eggplant, quartered (or regular eggplant cut into chunks)
- 1 red bell pepper, sliced
- Handful of Thai basil leaves
- Kaffir lime leaves, torn (optional)
- Fresh cilantro leaves, for garnish
- Cooked jasmine rice, for serving

Instructions:

1. **Prepare the Green Curry Paste:**
    - In a blender or food processor, combine green Thai chilies, shallots, garlic, lemongrass, galangal or ginger, cilantro stems, shrimp paste, ground coriander, ground cumin, ground white pepper, and kaffir lime zest (if using).
    - Blend until a smooth paste forms, adding vegetable oil as needed to help blend smoothly.
2. **Cooking the Curry:**

- Heat a large pot or deep skillet over medium heat. Add 2-3 tablespoons of green curry paste (adjust amount according to desired spiciness) and stir-fry for 1-2 minutes until fragrant.
- Add chicken pieces to the pot and stir to coat with the curry paste. Cook for 3-4 minutes until the chicken is lightly browned.
- Pour in coconut milk and chicken broth (or water). Stir well to combine.
- Add fish sauce and palm sugar (or brown sugar) to the pot. Stir again until the sugar is dissolved.
- Bring the curry to a simmer. Cook for 10-15 minutes, stirring occasionally, until the chicken is cooked through and tender.

3. **Add Vegetables and Herbs:**
   - Add Thai eggplant and red bell pepper to the pot. Simmer for another 5-7 minutes until the vegetables are tender.
   - Stir in torn kaffir lime leaves (if using) and Thai basil leaves. Simmer for another minute to infuse the flavors.

4. **Finish and Serve:**
   - Remove the pot from heat.
   - Taste and adjust the seasoning if needed, adding more fish sauce for saltiness or more sugar for sweetness.
   - Garnish with fresh cilantro leaves.

5. **Serve:**
   - Serve hot Thai Green Chicken Curry with steamed jasmine rice.

Tips:

- **Green Curry Paste:** Adjust the amount of green Thai chilies used according to your spice preference. Green curry paste can be stored in the refrigerator for up to 1 week or frozen for longer storage.
- **Vegetables:** Feel free to add other vegetables such as bamboo shoots, green beans, or zucchini.
- **Chicken:** Substitute chicken with tofu, shrimp, or beef for variations.

Kaeng Khiao Wan Kai is a comforting and aromatic Thai curry that combines the richness of coconut milk with the freshness of Thai herbs and spices. Enjoy preparing and savoring this delightful dish with friends and family!

Yum Talay (Spicy Thai Seafood Salad)

Ingredients:

For the Salad:

- 300g mixed seafood (shrimp, squid, mussels, scallops), cleaned and cooked
- 1 cup cherry tomatoes, halved
- 1/2 cup sliced red onion
- 1/2 cup sliced cucumber
- 1/4 cup chopped cilantro leaves
- 1/4 cup chopped green onions

For the Dressing:

- 3-4 bird's eye chilies, finely chopped (adjust to taste)
- 3 cloves garlic, minced
- 2 tablespoons fish sauce
- 2 tablespoons lime juice
- 1 tablespoon palm sugar or brown sugar
- 1 tablespoon roasted ground rice powder (optional)
- 1 tablespoon chopped cilantro stems

Optional Garnishes:

- Fresh cilantro leaves
- Thai basil leaves
- Roasted peanuts, crushed

Instructions:

1. **Prepare the Seafood:**
   - If using raw seafood, cook them by boiling in salted water until they are just cooked through. Drain and set aside to cool.
   - If using pre-cooked seafood, ensure they are thawed and ready to use.
2. **Make the Dressing:**
   - In a small bowl, combine chopped bird's eye chilies, minced garlic, fish sauce, lime juice, palm sugar (or brown sugar), roasted ground rice powder (if using), and chopped cilantro stems. Stir well until the sugar is dissolved.
3. **Assemble the Salad:**
   - In a large mixing bowl, combine cooked seafood, halved cherry tomatoes, sliced red onion, sliced cucumber, chopped cilantro leaves, and chopped green onions.
4. **Add the Dressing:**
   - Pour the prepared dressing over the seafood and vegetables in the bowl.
5. **Mix Well:**

- Gently toss all ingredients together until well combined and evenly coated with the dressing.

6. **Serve:**
    - Transfer the Yum Talay to a serving platter or individual plates.
    - Garnish with fresh cilantro leaves, Thai basil leaves, and crushed roasted peanuts if desired.

Tips:

- **Seafood:** Use a variety of seafood such as shrimp, squid, mussels, and scallops for a mix of textures and flavors.
- **Spice Level:** Adjust the amount of bird's eye chilies used according to your preference for spiciness.
- **Roasted Rice Powder:** To make roasted ground rice powder, dry roast uncooked jasmine rice in a skillet over medium heat until golden brown and fragrant. Grind it into a fine powder using a spice grinder or mortar and pestle.

Yum Talay is best served immediately after preparing to maintain its fresh and vibrant flavors. It makes a wonderful appetizer or main dish, perfect for sharing at a Thai-inspired meal!

Pla Nueng Manao (Steamed Fish with Lime and Chili)

Ingredients:

- 1 whole fish (such as sea bass or snapper), cleaned and scaled (about 500-600g)
- 3-4 cloves garlic, finely chopped
- 2-3 bird's eye chilies, thinly sliced (adjust to taste)
- 3 tablespoons fish sauce
- 3 tablespoons lime juice
- 1 tablespoon palm sugar or brown sugar
- 1/4 cup cilantro leaves, chopped
- 1/4 cup Thai basil leaves, chopped (optional)
- Fresh cilantro leaves, for garnish
- Lime slices, for garnish

Instructions:

1. **Prepare the Fish:**
   - Make 2-3 diagonal slashes on each side of the fish. This helps the flavors to penetrate during steaming.
2. **Prepare the Steamer:**
   - Fill a steamer pot with water and bring it to a boil over medium-high heat. Make sure the water level is below the steaming rack.
3. **Steam the Fish:**
   - Place the fish on a heatproof plate that fits inside your steamer basket. Steam the fish for 10-15 minutes, depending on the size and thickness of the fish, until it is cooked through and flakes easily with a fork.
4. **Make the Sauce:**
   - While the fish is steaming, prepare the sauce. In a small bowl, combine chopped garlic, sliced bird's eye chilies, fish sauce, lime juice, and palm sugar (or brown sugar). Stir well until the sugar is dissolved.
5. **Assemble the Dish:**
   - Once the fish is cooked, carefully remove it from the steamer and transfer it to a serving platter.
   - Pour the prepared sauce over the steamed fish, ensuring it covers the fish evenly.
6. **Garnish:**
   - Sprinkle chopped cilantro leaves and Thai basil leaves (if using) over the fish.
   - Garnish with fresh cilantro leaves and lime slices.
7. **Serve:**
   - Serve Pla Nueng Manao hot, accompanied by steamed jasmine rice.

Tips:

- **Choosing the Fish:** Whole fish such as sea bass or snapper are ideal for this dish due to their firm texture and mild flavor.
- **Steamer Alternatives:** If you don't have a steamer, you can steam the fish in a heatproof dish placed on a rack inside a large pot with a lid. Ensure there is enough water in the pot, and steam over medium heat.
- **Adjusting Flavor:** Adjust the amount of bird's eye chilies according to your spice preference. You can also add more lime juice or fish sauce to balance the flavors.

Pla Nueng Manao is a light and healthy Thai dish that showcases the natural sweetness of the fish complemented by the tangy and spicy sauce. It's perfect for a refreshing meal that's easy to prepare and full of vibrant flavors!

Pad Phak Boong Fai Daeng (Stir-Fried Morning Glory with Chili and Soy Bean Sauce)

Ingredients:

- 300g morning glory (also known as water spinach or kangkong), washed and trimmed
- 3-4 cloves garlic, minced
- 2-3 bird's eye chilies, thinly sliced (adjust to taste)
- 1 tablespoon fermented soybean paste (tao jiew)
- 1 tablespoon oyster sauce
- 1 tablespoon soy sauce
- 1 teaspoon sugar
- 1 tablespoon vegetable oil
- 1/4 cup water
- Thai jasmine rice, for serving

Instructions:

1. **Prepare the Morning Glory:**
   - Wash the morning glory thoroughly under cold water. Trim off any tough stems and cut into 3-inch lengths.
2. **Make the Sauce:**
   - In a small bowl, mix together fermented soybean paste (tao jiew), oyster sauce, soy sauce, and sugar. Stir well until the sugar is dissolved.
3. **Stir-Fry:**
   - Heat vegetable oil in a large skillet or wok over medium-high heat.
   - Add minced garlic and sliced bird's eye chilies. Stir-fry for about 30 seconds until fragrant.
   - Add the morning glory to the skillet. Stir-fry quickly for about 1-2 minutes until the morning glory starts to wilt.
4. **Add Sauce and Water:**
   - Pour the prepared sauce mixture over the morning glory in the skillet.
   - Add water to the skillet and continue to stir-fry for another 2-3 minutes until the morning glory is cooked through but still vibrant green and crunchy.
5. **Serve:**
   - Transfer the Stir-Fried Morning Glory to a serving dish.
   - Serve hot with steamed Thai jasmine rice.

Tips:

- **Morning Glory:** If you can't find morning glory, you can substitute with other leafy greens such as spinach or bok choy, though the taste will be slightly different.
- **Fermented Soybean Paste (Tao Jiew):** This ingredient adds a unique umami flavor to the dish. If you can't find it, you can substitute with miso paste or omit it if necessary.

- **Adjusting Spice Level:** Bird's eye chilies can be quite spicy. Adjust the amount according to your preference for spiciness.

Pad Phak Boong Fai Daeng is a quick and easy Thai vegetable dish that pairs well with jasmine rice or as a side dish to complement a larger Thai meal. Enjoy its fresh and savory flavors!

Pad Mee Korat (Spicy Stir-Fried Noodles from Korat)

Ingredients:

- 200g rice noodles (sen mee or thin rice noodles), soaked in warm water until softened
- 200g pork tenderloin or chicken breast, thinly sliced
- 3-4 cloves garlic, minced
- 2-3 bird's eye chilies, thinly sliced (adjust to taste)
- 1 cup mixed vegetables (carrots, bell peppers, snap peas), thinly sliced
- 2 tablespoons vegetable oil
- 1 tablespoon oyster sauce
- 1 tablespoon soy sauce
- 1 tablespoon fish sauce
- 1 tablespoon sugar
- 1/4 cup chicken broth or water
- Fresh cilantro leaves, for garnish
- Lime wedges, for serving

Instructions:

1. **Prepare the Rice Noodles:**
     - Soak the rice noodles in warm water according to package instructions until they are softened. Drain well and set aside.
2. **Stir-Fry:**
     - Heat vegetable oil in a large skillet or wok over medium-high heat.
     - Add minced garlic and sliced bird's eye chilies. Stir-fry for about 30 seconds until fragrant.
     - Add sliced pork or chicken to the skillet. Stir-fry for 2-3 minutes until the meat is cooked through.
3. **Add Vegetables:**
     - Add mixed vegetables (carrots, bell peppers, snap peas) to the skillet. Stir-fry for another 2-3 minutes until the vegetables are tender-crisp.
4. **Seasoning:**
     - In a small bowl, mix together oyster sauce, soy sauce, fish sauce, and sugar.
     - Pour the sauce mixture over the stir-fry in the skillet.
5. **Add Noodles:**
     - Add the softened rice noodles to the skillet. Toss everything together gently to combine and coat the noodles evenly with the sauce.
6. **Moisten with Broth:**
     - Add chicken broth or water to the skillet. Stir-fry for another 1-2 minutes until the noodles are heated through and well coated with the sauce.
7. **Serve:**
     - Transfer Pad Mee Korat to serving plates.

- Garnish with fresh cilantro leaves and serve immediately with lime wedges on the side.

Tips:

- **Noodles:** Use sen mee or thin rice noodles for an authentic texture. If using dried noodles, follow package instructions for soaking or cooking.
- **Protein:** Substitute pork or chicken with tofu, shrimp, or beef if desired.
- **Vegetables:** Feel free to customize the vegetables based on what you have available or prefer.

Pad Mee Korat is a spicy and savory noodle dish that makes a delicious and satisfying meal. Enjoy its bold flavors and the contrast of textures with each bite!

Khao Pad Sapparod (Pineapple Fried Rice)

Ingredients:

- 2 cups cooked jasmine rice, cooled (preferably day-old rice)
- 1 cup pineapple chunks, fresh or canned
- 200g chicken breast or shrimp, diced (optional)
- 2 eggs, beaten
- 1 small onion, diced
- 2-3 cloves garlic, minced
- 1/2 cup mixed vegetables (peas, carrots, bell peppers), diced
- 2 tablespoons vegetable oil
- 2 tablespoons fish sauce
- 1 tablespoon soy sauce
- 1 tablespoon oyster sauce
- 1 tablespoon curry powder
- 1/4 cup cashew nuts or peanuts, roasted (optional)
- Fresh cilantro leaves, for garnish
- Lime wedges, for serving

Instructions:

1. **Prepare the Ingredients:**
   - If using chicken breast or shrimp, dice them into small pieces.
   - Cook jasmine rice and allow it to cool. Day-old rice works best for fried rice as it's firmer and less sticky.
2. **Stir-Fry:**
   - Heat vegetable oil in a large skillet or wok over medium-high heat.
   - Add minced garlic and diced onion. Stir-fry for about 1 minute until fragrant.
   - If using chicken breast or shrimp, add them to the skillet. Cook until the chicken is no longer pink or the shrimp turns pink and opaque.
3. **Cook Eggs:**
   - Push the cooked chicken or shrimp to the side of the skillet. Pour beaten eggs into the empty space. Allow them to cook for a few seconds until they begin to set.
   - Scramble the eggs until fully cooked, then mix with the chicken or shrimp.
4. **Add Vegetables and Pineapple:**
   - Add diced mixed vegetables (peas, carrots, bell peppers) and pineapple chunks to the skillet. Stir-fry for about 2-3 minutes until the vegetables are tender-crisp.
5. **Seasoning:**
   - In a small bowl, mix together fish sauce, soy sauce, oyster sauce, and curry powder.
   - Pour the sauce mixture over the ingredients in the skillet. Stir to combine everything evenly.

6. **Add Rice:**
   - Add the cooled cooked jasmine rice to the skillet. Use a spatula to break up any clumps and mix well with the other ingredients.
7. **Finish and Serve:**
   - Stir-fry everything together for another 3-4 minutes until the rice is heated through and well coated with the sauce.
   - Taste and adjust seasoning if needed, adding more fish sauce or soy sauce if desired.
8. **Garnish and Serve:**
   - Remove the skillet from heat.
   - Garnish Khao Pad Sapparod with roasted cashew nuts or peanuts (if using) and fresh cilantro leaves.
   - Serve hot, with lime wedges on the side.

Tips:

- **Pineapple:** Fresh pineapple chunks work best for this dish, but you can also use canned pineapple chunks (drained well).
- **Protein:** Customize with chicken breast, shrimp, or even tofu for a vegetarian version.
- **Variations:** Feel free to add raisins, diced tomatoes, or other vegetables like corn or green beans for additional flavor and texture.

Khao Pad Sapparod is a colorful and aromatic dish that's perfect as a main course or as part of a larger Thai meal. Enjoy the sweet and savory flavors with each mouthful!

Khao Pad Gai (Thai Chicken Fried Rice)

Ingredients:

- 2 cups cooked jasmine rice, cooled (preferably day-old rice)
- 200g chicken breast, diced into small pieces
- 2 eggs, beaten
- 1 small onion, finely chopped
- 2-3 cloves garlic, minced
- 1/2 cup mixed vegetables (peas, carrots, bell peppers), diced
- 2 tablespoons vegetable oil
- 2 tablespoons fish sauce
- 1 tablespoon soy sauce
- 1 tablespoon oyster sauce
- 1 tablespoon sugar
- 1/4 teaspoon white pepper
- 1/4 cup green onions (scallions), chopped
- Fresh cilantro leaves, for garnish
- Lime wedges, for serving

Instructions:

1. **Prepare the Ingredients:**
   - Cook jasmine rice and allow it to cool. Day-old rice works best for fried rice as it's firmer and less sticky.
   - Dice the chicken breast into small pieces.
   - Beat the eggs in a small bowl.
2. **Stir-Fry:**
   - Heat vegetable oil in a large skillet or wok over medium-high heat.
   - Add minced garlic and finely chopped onion. Stir-fry for about 1 minute until fragrant.
3. **Cook Chicken:**
   - Add diced chicken breast to the skillet. Stir-fry until the chicken is cooked through and no longer pink.
4. **Add Vegetables and Eggs:**
   - Push the chicken to one side of the skillet. Pour beaten eggs into the empty space. Allow them to cook for a few seconds until they begin to set.
   - Scramble the eggs until fully cooked, then mix with the chicken.
5. **Combine Rice:**
   - Add diced mixed vegetables (peas, carrots, bell peppers) to the skillet. Stir-fry for about 2-3 minutes until the vegetables are tender-crisp.
   - Add the cooled cooked jasmine rice to the skillet. Use a spatula to break up any clumps and mix well with the other ingredients.
6. **Seasoning:**

- In a small bowl, mix together fish sauce, soy sauce, oyster sauce, sugar, and white pepper.
- Pour the sauce mixture over the ingredients in the skillet. Stir to combine everything evenly.

7. **Finish and Serve:**
   - Stir-fry everything together for another 3-4 minutes until the rice is heated through and well coated with the sauce.
   - Taste and adjust seasoning if needed.

8. **Garnish and Serve:**
   - Remove the skillet from heat.
   - Garnish Khao Pad Gai with chopped green onions (scallions) and fresh cilantro leaves.
   - Serve hot, with lime wedges on the side.

Tips:

- **Protein Options:** You can also use shrimp, pork, or tofu instead of chicken.
- **Vegetables:** Feel free to add other vegetables like corn, green beans, or broccoli florets.
- **Customization:** Adjust the amount of soy sauce, fish sauce, and sugar according to your taste preferences.

Khao Pad Gai is a classic Thai comfort food that's quick and easy to make at home. Enjoy its savory flavors and the contrast of textures with each bite!

Pad Thai Thale (Seafood Pad Thai)

Ingredients:

- 200g rice noodles (pad Thai noodles), soaked in warm water until softened
- 150g shrimp, peeled and deveined
- 150g squid, cleaned and sliced into rings
- 1/2 cup tofu, cut into small cubes (optional)
- 2 eggs, beaten
- 1 cup bean sprouts
- 1/2 cup chopped green onions (scallions)
- 1/4 cup crushed roasted peanuts
- 2 tablespoons vegetable oil
- 3 cloves garlic, minced
- 1 shallot, finely chopped
- 1/2 cup Pad Thai sauce (see recipe below)
- Lime wedges, for serving

Pad Thai Sauce:

- 3 tablespoons tamarind paste
- 3 tablespoons fish sauce
- 2 tablespoons soy sauce
- 2 tablespoons palm sugar or brown sugar
- 1/2 teaspoon chili powder (adjust to taste)

Instructions:

1. **Prepare the Pad Thai Sauce:**
   - In a small bowl, combine tamarind paste, fish sauce, soy sauce, palm sugar (or brown sugar), and chili powder. Stir well until the sugar is dissolved. Adjust the sweetness or spiciness according to your taste.
2. **Prepare the Ingredients:**
   - Soak rice noodles in warm water until softened, then drain and set aside.
   - Prepare shrimp, squid, tofu (if using), bean sprouts, chopped green onions, minced garlic, and finely chopped shallot.
3. **Stir-Fry:**
   - Heat vegetable oil in a large skillet or wok over medium-high heat.
   - Add minced garlic and chopped shallot. Stir-fry for about 1 minute until fragrant.
4. **Cook Seafood and Tofu:**
   - Add shrimp and squid to the skillet. Stir-fry for 2-3 minutes until shrimp turn pink and opaque and squid is cooked through.
   - If using tofu, add it to the skillet and stir-fry for another 1-2 minutes until heated through.

5. **Add Noodles and Eggs:**
    - Push the cooked seafood and tofu to one side of the skillet. Pour beaten eggs into the empty space. Allow them to cook for a few seconds until they begin to set.
    - Scramble the eggs until fully cooked, then mix with the seafood and tofu.
6. **Combine with Noodles:**
    - Add softened rice noodles to the skillet. Pour Pad Thai sauce over the noodles and toss everything together gently using tongs or chopsticks to coat the noodles evenly with the sauce.
7. **Add Bean Sprouts and Green Onions:**
    - Add bean sprouts and chopped green onions (scallions) to the skillet. Stir-fry for another 1-2 minutes until the bean sprouts are slightly wilted but still crunchy.
8. **Serve:**
    - Transfer Seafood Pad Thai to serving plates or a large platter.
    - Sprinkle crushed roasted peanuts over the top.
    - Serve hot with lime wedges on the side for squeezing over the noodles.

Tips:

- **Seafood:** You can use a combination of shrimp, squid, mussels, and scallops for variety.
- **Tofu:** Adds a vegetarian protein option. Make sure to press and dry tofu before using it in the dish.
- **Garnish:** Fresh cilantro leaves and additional bean sprouts can also be used for garnishing.

Enjoy this Seafood Pad Thai with its tangy, sweet, and savory flavors, perfect for a flavorful Thai meal at home!

Kao Pad Goong (Shrimp Fried Rice)

Ingredients:

- 2 cups cooked jasmine rice, cooled (preferably day-old rice)
- 200g shrimp, peeled and deveined
- 2 eggs, beaten
- 1 small onion, finely chopped
- 2-3 cloves garlic, minced
- 1/2 cup mixed vegetables (peas, carrots, bell peppers), diced
- 2 tablespoons vegetable oil
- 2 tablespoons fish sauce
- 1 tablespoon soy sauce
- 1 tablespoon oyster sauce
- 1 tablespoon sugar
- 1/4 teaspoon white pepper
- 1/4 cup green onions (scallions), chopped
- Fresh cilantro leaves, for garnish
- Lime wedges, for serving

Instructions:

1. **Prepare the Ingredients:**
   - Cook jasmine rice and allow it to cool. Day-old rice works best for fried rice as it's firmer and less sticky.
   - Peel and devein shrimp if not already prepared.
   - Beat the eggs in a small bowl.
2. **Stir-Fry:**
   - Heat vegetable oil in a large skillet or wok over medium-high heat.
   - Add minced garlic and finely chopped onion. Stir-fry for about 1 minute until fragrant.
3. **Cook Shrimp:**
   - Add shrimp to the skillet. Stir-fry until shrimp are pink and opaque, about 2-3 minutes. Remove shrimp from skillet and set aside.
4. **Cook Eggs:**
   - Push cooked shrimp to the side of the skillet. Pour beaten eggs into the empty space. Allow them to cook for a few seconds until they begin to set.
   - Scramble the eggs until fully cooked, then mix with the shrimp.
5. **Add Vegetables and Rice:**
   - Add diced mixed vegetables (peas, carrots, bell peppers) to the skillet. Stir-fry for about 2-3 minutes until vegetables are tender-crisp.
   - Add the cooled cooked jasmine rice to the skillet. Use a spatula to break up any clumps and mix well with the other ingredients.
6. **Seasoning:**

- In a small bowl, mix together fish sauce, soy sauce, oyster sauce, sugar, and white pepper.
- Pour the sauce mixture over the ingredients in the skillet. Stir to combine everything evenly.

7. **Finish and Serve:**
   - Stir-fry everything together for another 3-4 minutes until the rice is heated through and well coated with the sauce.
   - Taste and adjust seasoning if needed.

8. **Garnish and Serve:**
   - Remove the skillet from heat.
   - Garnish Kao Pad Goong with chopped green onions (scallions) and fresh cilantro leaves.
   - Serve hot, with lime wedges on the side.

Tips:

- **Variations:** Feel free to add additional vegetables like corn, green beans, or broccoli florets.
- **Protein Options:** Substitute shrimp with chicken, pork, or tofu for variation.
- **Customization:** Adjust the amount of soy sauce, fish sauce, and sugar according to your taste preferences.

Enjoy this delicious and simple Thai Shrimp Fried Rice with its savory flavors and delightful textures!

Gaeng Som Pla (Thai Spicy and Sour Fish Curry)

Ingredients:

- 500g firm white fish fillets (such as snapper or cod), cut into bite-sized pieces
- 2 cups water or fish stock
- 2 tablespoons fish sauce
- 2 tablespoons tamarind paste
- 2 tablespoons palm sugar or brown sugar
- 2-3 Thai bird's eye chilies, chopped (adjust to taste)
- 1 tablespoon shrimp paste (kapi)
- 1 cup mixed vegetables (such as bamboo shoots, long beans, eggplant), sliced
- 1 tomato, cut into wedges
- Handful of Thai basil leaves
- Fresh cilantro leaves, for garnish
- Lime wedges, for serving

Paste (Curry Paste):

- 5-6 dried red chilies, soaked in hot water until softened
- 3 cloves garlic, peeled
- 1 shallot, peeled and chopped
- 1 lemongrass stalk, white part only, chopped
- 1-inch piece of galangal, sliced
- 1 teaspoon shrimp paste (kapi)
- 1 teaspoon ground turmeric
- 1 tablespoon vegetable oil

Instructions:

1. **Prepare the Curry Paste:**
   - In a mortar and pestle, pound the soaked dried red chilies, garlic, shallot, lemongrass, galangal, shrimp paste, and ground turmeric into a smooth paste. Alternatively, use a food processor to blend until smooth.
2. **Cooking the Curry:**
   - Heat vegetable oil in a large pot over medium heat. Add the curry paste and fry for 2-3 minutes until fragrant.
   - Add water or fish stock to the pot. Bring to a boil.
   - Stir in fish sauce, tamarind paste, and palm sugar. Adjust the sweetness and sourness according to your taste preference.
3. **Add Vegetables and Fish:**
   - Add mixed vegetables (bamboo shoots, long beans, eggplant) to the pot. Simmer for 5-7 minutes until vegetables are tender.

- Add fish fillet pieces and tomato wedges to the pot. Cook for another 5-7 minutes until fish is cooked through and flakes easily with a fork.
4. **Final Touches:**
   - Stir in Thai bird's eye chilies (adjust amount based on desired spiciness) and Thai basil leaves. Remove from heat.
5. **Serve:**
   - Garnish Gaeng Som Pla with fresh cilantro leaves.
   - Serve hot with steamed jasmine rice and lime wedges on the side.

Tips:

- **Fish Selection:** Use firm white fish fillets that hold their shape well when cooked.
- **Spiciness:** Adjust the amount of Thai bird's eye chilies based on your preference for heat.
- **Vegetables:** Feel free to add other vegetables like pumpkin, zucchini, or mushrooms.

Gaeng Som Pla is a vibrant and aromatic Thai curry that combines the tangy flavors of tamarind and the heat of chilies with the delicate sweetness of fish. Enjoy its bold flavors and comforting warmth!

Pad Pak Ruam (Stir-Fried Mixed Vegetables)

Ingredients:

- 2 cups mixed vegetables (such as broccoli florets, bell peppers, carrots, snow peas, baby corn, mushrooms, etc.), cut into bite-sized pieces
- 2 tablespoons vegetable oil
- 2-3 cloves garlic, minced
- 1 small onion, thinly sliced
- 1 red chili, thinly sliced (optional, for heat)
- 2 tablespoons oyster sauce
- 1 tablespoon soy sauce (or to taste)
- 1 tablespoon fish sauce (optional, for extra umami)
- 1 tablespoon sugar
- Freshly ground black pepper, to taste
- Fresh cilantro leaves, for garnish (optional)
- Lime wedges, for serving

Instructions:

1. **Prepare the Vegetables:**
    - Wash and cut the mixed vegetables into bite-sized pieces. You can use a combination of broccoli florets, bell peppers, carrots, snow peas, baby corn, mushrooms, or any other vegetables you prefer.
2. **Stir-Fry:**
    - Heat vegetable oil in a large skillet or wok over medium-high heat.
    - Add minced garlic and thinly sliced onion to the skillet. Stir-fry for about 1 minute until fragrant.
3. **Add Vegetables:**
    - Add the harder vegetables (like carrots or broccoli) to the skillet first. Stir-fry for 2-3 minutes until they start to soften slightly.
    - Add the remaining vegetables and red chili (if using). Stir-fry for another 2-3 minutes until all the vegetables are tender-crisp.
4. **Seasoning:**
    - In a small bowl, mix together oyster sauce, soy sauce, fish sauce (if using), sugar, and freshly ground black pepper.
    - Pour the sauce mixture over the vegetables in the skillet. Stir well to coat all the vegetables evenly with the sauce.
5. **Finish and Serve:**
    - Continue stir-frying for another 1-2 minutes until the vegetables are heated through and well coated with the sauce.
    - Taste and adjust seasoning if needed, adding more soy sauce or sugar according to your preference.
6. **Garnish and Serve:**

- Remove the skillet from heat.
- Garnish Pad Pak Ruam with fresh cilantro leaves (if using).
- Serve hot, with lime wedges on the side for squeezing over the vegetables.

Tips:

- **Vegetable Selection:** Use a variety of colorful vegetables for visual appeal and different textures.
- **Customization:** Feel free to adjust the amount of sauce ingredients based on your taste preferences.
- **Protein Addition:** You can add tofu, chicken, shrimp, or beef to make it a more substantial main dish.

Pad Pak Ruam is a versatile and nutritious dish that can be enjoyed on its own as a vegetarian meal or as a side dish to complement other Thai dishes. Enjoy its vibrant flavors and crunchy textures!

Kai Jeow (Thai Omelette)

Ingredients:

- 2-3 large eggs
- 1 tablespoon fish sauce
- 1 tablespoon soy sauce
- 1 tablespoon oyster sauce (optional)
- 1/4 teaspoon ground white pepper
- Vegetable oil, for frying
- Fresh cilantro leaves or green onions, chopped, for garnish (optional)
- Thai chili sauce or Sriracha, for serving (optional)

Instructions:

1. **Prepare the Egg Mixture:**
   - In a bowl, crack the eggs and beat them lightly with a fork or whisk.
   - Add fish sauce, soy sauce, oyster sauce (if using), and ground white pepper to the beaten eggs. Mix well until everything is combined.
2. **Heat Oil:**
   - Heat vegetable oil in a non-stick skillet or frying pan over medium-high heat. The amount of oil should be enough to cover the bottom of the pan generously.
3. **Fry the Omelette:**
   - Once the oil is hot (but not smoking), pour the egg mixture into the skillet. It should sizzle immediately around the edges.
   - Tilt the skillet to spread the egg mixture evenly across the pan. Allow it to cook undisturbed for about 1-2 minutes until the bottom is golden brown and crispy.
4. **Flip and Cook:**
   - Carefully flip the omelette using a spatula. Cook the other side for another 1-2 minutes until golden brown and cooked through.
5. **Serve:**
   - Transfer the Kai Jeow to a serving plate lined with paper towels to absorb excess oil.
   - Garnish with fresh cilantro leaves or chopped green onions, if desired.
   - Serve hot with jasmine rice and Thai chili sauce or Sriracha on the side for dipping.

Tips:

- **Crispy Texture:** For a crispier omelette, use enough oil and allow it to get hot before adding the egg mixture.
- **Variations:** You can add chopped onions, tomatoes, or green chilies to the egg mixture for added flavor and texture.

- **Dipping Sauce:** Thai sweet chili sauce or a squeeze of lime juice with a dash of fish sauce and chopped chilies makes an excellent dipping sauce.

Kai Jeow is a quick and satisfying dish that's enjoyed for its simplicity and versatility. It pairs wonderfully with steamed rice and other Thai dishes, or even as a standalone snack. Enjoy your homemade Thai omelette!

Pad Cha (Spicy Stir-Fry with Thai Herbs)

Ingredients:

- 300g chicken, beef, pork, or shrimp, thinly sliced or diced
- 2 tablespoons vegetable oil
- 3-4 cloves garlic, minced
- 1-2 Thai bird's eye chilies, finely chopped (adjust to taste)
- 1 red bell pepper, sliced
- 1 onion, sliced
- 1 cup Thai holy basil leaves (or regular basil if unavailable)
- 1 tablespoon fish sauce
- 1 tablespoon soy sauce
- 1 tablespoon oyster sauce
- 1 tablespoon sugar
- 1/2 cup mixed vegetables (optional, such as baby corn, mushrooms, snap peas)
- Fresh lime wedges, for serving
- Fresh cilantro leaves, for garnish

Paste (Curry Paste):

- 5-6 dried red chilies, soaked in hot water until softened
- 3 cloves garlic, peeled
- 1 shallot, peeled and chopped
- 1 lemongrass stalk, white part only, chopped
- 1-inch piece of galangal, sliced
- 1 kaffir lime zest (or substitute with lime zest)
- 1 teaspoon shrimp paste (kapi)
- 1 teaspoon ground white pepper
- 1 tablespoon vegetable oil

Instructions:

1. **Prepare the Curry Paste:**
   - In a mortar and pestle, pound the soaked dried red chilies, garlic, shallot, lemongrass, galangal, kaffir lime zest, shrimp paste, and ground white pepper into a smooth paste. Alternatively, use a food processor to blend until smooth.
2. **Stir-Fry:**
   - Heat vegetable oil in a large skillet or wok over medium-high heat.
   - Add minced garlic and the prepared curry paste to the skillet. Stir-fry for about 1-2 minutes until fragrant.
3. **Add Meat or Seafood:**
   - Add the thinly sliced or diced meat (chicken, beef, pork, or shrimp) to the skillet. Stir-fry until the meat is almost cooked through.

4. **Vegetables and Seasoning:**
    - Add sliced red bell pepper, onion, and mixed vegetables (if using) to the skillet. Stir-fry for another 2-3 minutes until the vegetables are tender-crisp.
    - Stir in fish sauce, soy sauce, oyster sauce, and sugar. Mix well to coat all ingredients with the sauce.
5. **Finish and Serve:**
    - Add Thai holy basil leaves (or regular basil) to the skillet. Stir-fry for another 1-2 minutes until the basil leaves are wilted.
    - Remove from heat and transfer Pad Cha to a serving dish.
6. **Garnish and Serve:**
    - Garnish with fresh cilantro leaves.
    - Serve hot with steamed jasmine rice and fresh lime wedges on the side.

Tips:

- **Spiciness:** Adjust the amount of Thai bird's eye chilies according to your spice tolerance.
- **Variations:** Feel free to customize with your choice of protein and vegetables.
- **Herbs:** Thai holy basil is traditionally used for its unique flavor, but regular basil can be substituted if needed.

Pad Cha is a vibrant and aromatic Thai dish that's perfect for those who enjoy bold and spicy flavors. Enjoy this delicious stir-fry with its fragrant herbs and savory sauce!

Khao Mun Gai (Thai Chicken Rice)

Ingredients:

For the Chicken:

- 4 chicken thighs or chicken breasts (bone-in and skin-on)
- 4 slices ginger
- 4 cloves garlic, crushed
- 2 stalks spring onions, cut into segments
- 1 tablespoon soy sauce
- 1 tablespoon oyster sauce
- 1 teaspoon sugar
- Salt and pepper, to taste

For the Rice:

- 2 cups jasmine rice
- 2 cups chicken broth (from cooking the chicken)
- 4 cloves garlic, minced
- 1 tablespoon vegetable oil
- Salt, to taste

For the Sauce:

- 1/4 cup soy sauce
- 1/4 cup chicken broth (from cooking the chicken)
- 2 tablespoons ginger, finely minced
- 2 tablespoons garlic, finely minced
- 2 tablespoons vinegar (rice vinegar or white vinegar)
- 1 tablespoon sugar
- 1 teaspoon sesame oil
- Thai chili sauce or Sriracha, to taste (optional)

For Garnish:

- Fresh cucumber slices
- Fresh cilantro leaves
- Fresh spring onions, chopped

Instructions:

1. **Cook the Chicken:**
    - In a large pot, bring water to a boil. Add ginger slices, crushed garlic, spring onions, soy sauce, oyster sauce, sugar, salt, and pepper.

- Add the chicken thighs or breasts to the pot and simmer gently over medium heat for about 20-25 minutes, or until the chicken is cooked through (internal temperature should reach 165°F or 74°C).
    - Once cooked, remove the chicken from the pot and let it cool. Reserve the chicken broth for cooking the rice.
2. **Cook the Rice:**
    - Rinse jasmine rice under cold water until the water runs clear. Drain well.
    - Heat vegetable oil in a large saucepan over medium heat. Add minced garlic and sauté until fragrant.
    - Add the rinsed rice to the saucepan and stir-fry for 1-2 minutes.
    - Pour in the reserved chicken broth (about 2 cups) and bring to a boil. Reduce heat to low, cover, and simmer for 15-20 minutes, or until the rice is cooked and all liquid is absorbed. Remove from heat and let it rest, covered, for 5 minutes.
3. **Prepare the Sauce:**
    - In a small saucepan, combine soy sauce, chicken broth, minced ginger, minced garlic, vinegar, sugar, and sesame oil. Bring to a simmer over low heat and cook for 3-4 minutes until slightly thickened. Remove from heat and set aside.
4. **Assemble and Serve:**
    - Once the chicken has cooled slightly, remove the skin and bones. Slice or shred the chicken into bite-sized pieces.
    - Serve Khao Mun Gai by placing a generous portion of the cooked rice on each plate. Arrange the sliced/shredded chicken on top.
    - Drizzle the prepared sauce over the chicken and rice.
    - Garnish with fresh cucumber slices, cilantro leaves, and chopped spring onions.
    - Serve immediately with Thai chili sauce or Sriracha on the side, if desired.

Tips:

- **Rice Consistency:** The rice should be fragrant and slightly sticky, but not mushy. Adjust the cooking time and amount of broth accordingly.
- **Chicken:** You can use boneless chicken breasts or thighs if preferred, but bone-in and skin-on chicken tends to be more flavorful.
- **Sauce:** Adjust the sweetness and acidity of the sauce to your taste preference by adding more or less sugar and vinegar.

Khao Mun Gai is a comforting and satisfying dish that highlights the delicate flavors of chicken and rice, complemented by the savory ginger-garlic sauce. Enjoy this classic Thai street food at home!

www.ingramcontent.com/pod-product-compliance
Lightning Source LLC
LaVergne TN
LVHW081559060526
838201LV00054B/1965